Recommendations for
Delivering and Measuring Customer Service

"As a student and teacher of the subject, this is the finest book on customer service I've ever read. Why? It's so practical, so down to earth – beautifully bridging theory and principles with techniques and practices. A literal treasure trove of doable ideas!"
—Stephen R. Covey
Author, The 7 Habits of Highly Effective People, and
The 8th Habit: From Effectiveness to Greatness

"If you are interested in customer service this is must reading. If you are not, this will convert you now. Useful, applicable, and fun. I learned a lot."
—William R. Tiefel
Chairman, CarMax, Inc.
Chairman Emeritus, The Ritz-Carlton Hotel Company, LLC

"A commitment to delivering and measuring customer service is the hallmark of truly great companies. Rich Hanks has captured the heart of that commitment with his down-to-earth writing style. This book is full of actionable insights that can be put into practice today."
—Nolan D. Archibald
Chairman and CEO, Black & Decker

"JetBlue isn't in the aviation business; we're in the customer service business. People ask us where we get our innovative service ideas and the answer is simple, our customers tell us what they want, and we deliver. That is what Hanks' book is all about."
—David Neeleman
Founder and Former Chairman, JetBlue Airways

"Fulfilling the expectations of customers – past, present, and future – is a key to profitable innovation. This book coaches corporate leaders, not only on 'why,' but 'how' to do that."
—Clayton M. Christensen
Professor of Business Administration, Harvard Business School
Author, The Innovator's Dilemma

Finally – a book that focuses on the practicalities and common sense of taking care of customers, measuring their experiences, and taking tactical actions to improve!

"It's refreshing to read a business book that is both relevant and entertaining. The techniques you share have been proven to not only build sales, but also create loyal followers that are faithful to a brand. The days of actually listening, learning and responding to customers are back!"
> **—John D. Barr**
> *CEO,* Papa Murphy's International

"This is a great book. It is packed full of relevant and fun insights. Rich Hanks also communicates these tried and tested principles in a way that instantly strikes a chord with operators. Well done!"
> **—Bob Nilsen**
> *CEO,* Cafe Rio
> *Former President,* Burger King

"This book is the standard for every executive dedicated to continuously improving their operations, and a must read for everyone in the organization. Hanks provides the reader with a little bit of theory, a large amount of relevant, real world solutions, and a dose of humor."
> **—Robert H. Garff**
> *Chairman and CEO,* Garff Enterprises
> *Chair,* Salt Lake Olympic Organizing Committee

"It's easy to talk about superior customer service – it is another thing to consistently deliver it. This book hits the nail on the head when it positions measurement of the actual customer experience as the driving force behind operations improvement. We've seen it work in our company."
> **—Ken Cole**
> *President and CEO,* Quaker Steak and Lube
> *Former President and CEO,* Sizzler USA

"A tremendously valuable tool for any executive who is clearly devoted to raising the quality of the customer experience and enhancing customer delight. We've seen the positive results of utilizing the principles taught in this exciting book and recommend them highly."
> **—Larry J. Magee**
> *Chairman and CEO,* Bridgestone Firestone Retail and Commercial Operations

Delivering and Measuring Customer Service

This isn't rocket surgery!

**Practical reflections on the most important
thing your business can do**

Richard D. Hanks

Duff Road Endeavors
Salt Lake City, Utah

Duff Road Endeavors
310 East 4500 South, #450, Salt Lake City, UT 84107
Printed in the United States of America
www.duffroad.com

First Edition: May 2008
Second Edition: March 2010

Library of Congress Control Number: 2009943336
ISBN: 978-0-578-04604-4

Disclaimer
The principles outlined in this book are being practiced at hundreds of
successful companies. While every effort has been made to make this
book as complete and as accurate as possible, no warranty or fitness is
implied. The information provided is on an "as is" basis. The author and
the publisher shall have neither liability nor responsibility to any person
or entity with respect to any loss or damages arising from the information
itself, or use of the information contained in this book.

Every effort has been made to give attribution to original source materials.
If any have been missed, please let the author or publisher know for
future editions. If there are omissions, there is no intent to take credit for
another's work, rather lack of knowledge of original authorship.

Designed by Robert McAllister

Except as indicated, artwork is by Ted Goff, Robert McAllister, Mark
Anderson, and Carl Rose. All cartoons and artwork are used with
permission.

Dedication

To my wonderful wife and best friend, Liz,
and to my Mom and Dad.

They exemplify the best kind of customer service,
which is Christ-like love for others.

Acknowledgments

I'd like to acknowledge a few of the people who made this book possible. Thank you to John Sperry, my partner at Mindshare, for his friendship, intellect, passion, and perseverance. To Robert McAllister, who can take any idea for a chart, advertisement, picture, or illustration, and make it "sing." To Brad Clark and Kurt Williams for their dependability and reliability. To John Crofts, Robert Walker, and Aubrie Hicks who helped me sweat the grammatical details. To Lonnie Mayne, Chad Hortin, Erich Dietz, Shane Evans, Tyler Rees, and the rest of the Mindshare team who read through the various drafts and provided important feedback. To Ted Goff for permission to use his wonderful cartoons. And all my love to Emily Hanks Aldrich, Daniel D. Hanks, and Katherine S. Hanks, my most demanding, yet rewarding, "customers" and my brightest hope for the future.

I'd also like to thank the executives and team members of Mindshare who live what they preach day in and day out. Thank you to the many executives of hundreds of companies who are committed to the long-term satisfaction and loyalty of their customers and employees, and who demonstrate that long-term commitment by their daily actions and their allocation of resources. And hats off to the individual men and women around the world who provide daily service in jobs where strategy and vision statements evaporate and it all comes down to a couple of human beings interacting with each other in a terrific service experience.

Since I don't know if I'll ever write another book, I'd also like to pay special tribute to a few additional folks who have strongly influenced my business life. To my father, Marion D. Hanks, who demonstrated through his life how true servant-leaders behave and why integrity is paramount; to Professor R. DerMont Bell, who in one ruthless (but appreciated) semester, taught me how to write for business; to Mac Christensen, who taught me how to sell; to Carol Ediger and LaMarr W. Poulton, who believed in me; and to my good friend Steve Weisz, who has mentored me since my earliest days at Marriott, and who taught me about business execution, diplomacy, and success.

Contents

Table of Contents

Introduction

Have you ever had such a lousy customer service experience that you wanted to smack your server upside the head? It may have been in a restaurant or clothing store, on an airplane, or on a phone call. Perhaps the employee ignored you, acted uninterested, or made a mistake but didn't even know it. Or, maybe the product wasn't up to snuff or the atmosphere wasn't pleasant. You've been there; you know what I mean. But what if this is happening today at your company, with your products, and your employees? Would you know? Would you be able to react? Would you be able to recover the customer before you lose him or her forever?

Here's a favorite story: One day, a young man, we'll call Bob, began as a waiter at a seafood restaurant. His first night on the job, the restaurant's feedback system recorded a customer complaining that the clam chowder he had ordered didn't contain any clams. No one had taught Bob that clams sink to the bottom of the pot if not stirred frequently. Ignorant to this fact, Bob was serving bowls of chowder without any clams. Based on the feedback, the restaurant quickly adjusted its training program to include teaching employees to stir the clam chowder before serving, and solved the problem.

In addition, the restaurant was able to effect immediate service-lapse recovery by contacting the affected customers, apologizing, explaining how the problem had been fixed, and inviting them to return for a complimentary meal. The restaurant's customers, in effect, became "performance coaches" for front-line staff, leading to both customer retention and increased profits. The practical outcome of this story epitomizes my hope for this book.

This book focuses on the common sense of taking care of customers, measuring their experiences, and taking actions to improve. There are three simple themes I hope you take away. They are:

1. **Customer retention is *as important*, if not *more important*, than customer acquisition.** It costs substantially more to acquire a new customer than to keep an existing one.

2. ***Delivering* exceptional customer service and *measuring* customer satisfaction are *no longer optional*.** Winning companies are doing it, and doing it well – and you'd better be doing it if you want to compete. Customers expect it, and believe they have a "right" to it.

3. **Strategy is helpful, but *execution* is *paramount*!** All the late-night strategy sessions and all of the brilliant ideas you've had will amount to exactly zero if you don't perform day in and day out. As a consumer, have you ever "fired" a bank, a pizza parlor, or a doctor who didn't meet your expectation? Of course you have. The consumer is in charge. He demands near-perfect execution.

In industries from banking to airlines, from office supplies to the global carmakers – customer choice has morphed from Henry Ford's choose "any color Model T, as long as it's black," to options, styles, and alternatives galore. Consumers are presented with an incredible array of product and service choices and they will make themselves heard if each experience is not top-notch.

At the same time, leading-edge service companies have shown customers that exceptional service *is* possible in all areas. This has not only set a precedent ***within*** industries, but ***across*** industries. As a consumer, I no longer compare a restaurant's knowledge about me only to other restaurant chains, but across other industries as well. For example, how can a well-known retailer know how to spell my street name, but my phone company can't? Problem resolution in the car rental industry must now compete with Nordstrom, where the customer can get products replaced without question. When I call to make a travel reservation, why do I have to provide my name over and over again, when my bank knows my information as soon as they answer the phone? On the other hand, why does the bank need to transfer me to different specialists, when a Ritz-Carlton housekeeper will stop what she's doing and walk me down to the restaurant I just inquired about?

Customers now feel they have a "right" to exceptional service and absolute satisfaction, which will determine where their money flows. The good news for providers is that the answers are not all that difficult. They lie within our *existing processes* and our ***existing employees***. **They lie in the fundamentals!**

One of the most basic fundamentals is a willingness to **listen to customers tell their side of the story**, even if we don't like what they have to say.

It is imperative that we have the humility to listen to and acknowledge our weaknesses, and that we are totally dedicated to continuously improve our business. The cartoons on the following page sum up this topic nicely.

*We think we know what the customer is experiencing...
But do we really?*

"Our customers have told us that
everything we do is wrong.
Therefore, we need new customers."

So, this is a book about ***basics***. You won't find one single equation like this:

$$y = {}^\wedge y\,\eta + \varepsilon$$

This is a "how-to" book, not a book for rocket scientists or brain surgeons
- hence the title. It is intended to be practical, realistic, and full of common
sense. My goal is to present the case for you to: (1) <u>put customers first</u> in your
company, (2) <u>commit</u> to ongoing, continuous customer and employee satisfaction
measurement, and (3) <u>use</u> that feedback to continuously improve your operations.

If you prefer academic detail or more specialized training, may I suggest you
read some of my favorite customer service titles listed in the *References and
Recommended Reading* section (page 197) at the end of the book. Each of the
wonderful authors listed there has helped shape my approach in listening to,
and serving customers. Their insights have influenced, both consciously and
subconsciously, the contents of this book.

Why is this book about ***tactics*** and ***execution***, rather than strategy and academics?
Because my experience has led me to conclude that significantly ***more companies
are failing due to poor execution than are failing due to poor strategy.***

My business partner, John Sperry, and I both love to paraphrase the famous
American General, George S. Patton:

"A good plan violently executed now is better than a perfect plan next week."

Our own company's success has come from our unwavering passion for
"violent execution" and practicing what we preach. Because Mindshare was a
bootstrapped company, we couldn't afford to hire customer service people for
the first couple of years, so most of the current executive team did it ourselves.
The time we spend personally helping clients and customers has ingrained in
us a service culture that has made us all the more responsive. We grasp every
piece of feedback we can get our hands on. We want to be known as good
listeners who follow through. We've personally tested all the principles presented
herein. This guidebook summarizes the grass roots, detailed tactics that will
help your company – and more importantly, your customers – succeed.

Richard Duff Hanks

Richard D. Hanks

Using this book

Suggestions on getting the most from your reading

Once through, quickly

Read through the book quickly from cover to cover.

(I've tried to make it an "easy read," by including some interesting titles, light-hearted stories, real-life examples and a laugh or two along the way.)

For now, skip the "Practical Tactics: (Questions to ponder)" box at the end of each chapter, and all of the sections at the end of the book.

Jot down big ideas that stand out to you.

Once more, with application to your situation

Now, read it again with your team or leadership group.

This time, skim the chapters, but STOP at the end of each chapter and carefully read the "Practical Tactics (Questions to ponder)" box at the end of each chapter.

Ask yourself each question out loud – and answer each one. Do you like your answers? Where is your organization weak? Strong? Trending up? Falling down?

Draft a list of ideas that you can attack RIGHT NOW!

Focus on three or four areas where you feel that you can personally make a difference. Set goals. Commit to taking action.

Second edition updates

This updated edition amplifies several areas that have evolved since the first printing, including social media feedback (structuring the unstructured), measuring the return on investment, and utilizing enterprise feedback management tools. I have also added a few additional examples, corrected some errors, rewritten a few sections, added some newly discovered attributions, and updated charts and graphs.

Feedback

Please feel free to provide me with feedback (both uplifting and constructive). I view the book as a "work in progress" and welcome your input.

Delivering and Measuring Customer Service

This isn't rocket surgery!

**Practical reflections on the most important
thing your business can do**

Part I

General Overview

Loyalty and measurement:

Two main principles of success

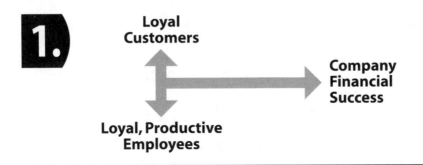

1. Loyal Customers — Company Financial Success — Loyal, Productive Employees

2. **That which gets measured one-time improves.**

That which gets measured <u>continuously</u> improves exponentially.

My experience in delivering and measuring customer service can be summarized in the two main principles shown above:

1. The *first principle** is that the major drivers of a company's financial success can be traced back to:

   • Truly *loyal customers* who return and recommend your business over and over, and who become your most profitable "assets," and

   • *Loyal employees* who, through their longevity and experience, become increasingly more *productive,* thereby providing better service and contributing even more to the company's bottom line.

2. The *second principle* is rather simple: Measure your customers' experience *continuously.* Organizations committed to continuous improvement understand that "there is no finish line" in customer service. You need to take your customers' pulse daily. (If you only gather customer feedback sporadically, you are seeing only a partial view of the business.) Just asking for feedback is, itself, a loyalty-generating activity, assuming the company acts on what it has learned. Delivering and measuring terrific customer service is not a fad or a program or a trend – *it should be how you approach your business, every day.*

* (This has been borne out through numerous studies. My favorite is, "Putting the Service-Profit Chain to Work," by Heskett, et al., Harvard Business Review, March-April, 1994.)

Customer Expectations

Closing customer delivery gaps

I had to laugh at a sign I saw the other day over the cash register in a local store. It read:

> ## **Quality.   Service.   Price.**
> ### *(Choose any two)*

I had a good chuckle until I thought seriously about what it meant. You see, this kind of thinking just doesn't work any more. As customers, we want it all. However, we are often disappointed. Why? What makes up our disappointment? Is it possible to investigate the causes of our disappointment and analyze them further?

A relatively simple way is to start with the expectations, or ***promises*** set between a company and its customers. For example:

- We set promises with our marketing and advertising.
- We set promises through past customer experiences.
- We set promises through what others say about us.

These promises create ***expectations.*** Those expectations are either met or not met, depending upon what the customer perceives he received. Businesses that are truly interested in becoming customer-centric will want customers to express their dissatisfaction and disappointments about expectations vs. execution.

Here are three basic ways of looking at service delivery measurement:

1. Dave Power III of J.D. Power and Associates is quoted as saying, "When we measure satisfaction, what we're really measuring is the difference between what a customer ***expects,*** and what a customer ***perceives*** he gets."*

$$\text{Customer Satisfaction} = \text{What customer expects to get} - \text{What customer perceives he gets}$$

* (Quoted in "The Experience Economy," by B. Joseph Pine II and James H. Gilmore, HBS Press, 1999.)

2. In their book, *The Experience Economy,* Pine and Gilmore take it one step further to define "Customer Sacrifice."* They define Customer Sacrifice as a concept describing the difference between what a customer *wanted* and what a customer *settled* for. In other words:

Customer Sacrifice **=** **What customer wants exactly** **−** **What customer settles for**

3. Services marketing writings often include a discussion of managing specific service deficiencies, or gaps.** One example is the gap between what a company has *promised* the customer and what the company *delivers*.

An example gap

Customer Service Deficiencies **=** **What a company has promised** **−** **What a company delivers**

The key learnings for me in each of these formulas are: (1) the presence of a *gap* between the company and the customer – the distance between a promise/expectation and *poor execution,* and (2) the *inaccuracy of the promise/expectation* to begin with. I'll leave it up to others to explore the details of correctly setting company promises (mostly through branding and advertising) and specific methods of service delivery (mostly through hiring, training, and operations process). In this book we will focus primarily on understanding what the customers' expectations are, determining how they felt about their experience, and listening to their feedback to gain measurement on our execution.

Before moving our focus to measuring customer satisfaction and delivering top-notch execution, let me summarize some of my basic rules-of-thumb on setting customer expectations.

* *(From "The Experience Economy," by B. Joseph Pine II and James H. Gilmore, HBS Press, 1999.)*

** *(For example, see "Delivering Quality Service: Balancing Customer Perceptions and Expectations," by Zeithaml, Parasuraman & Berry, The Free Press, 1990.)*

Rich's Rules on Setting Expectations

- It is always better to under-promise and over-deliver.
- Never lie to a customer (not overtly, nor accidentally).
- Always "pad" delivery times and costs to plan for the unexpected.
- If you're not going to be able to deliver on a promise, tell them now!
- Accept blame for mistakes. Say, "I'm sorry," and immediately fix the problem.
- Transparency is the new "norm" in business. Tell your customers what you are doing. Communicate. Communicate. Communicate.

Now, let's return back to the gaps between you and your customers.

Closing customer service gaps is a lot like any personal reformation effort:

- First, we need to **admit** we've got a problem and determine to improve.
- Second, we **plan** how we'll close the gap.
- Third, we put in measurable **metrics to monitor** our progress.
- Fourth, we constantly **adjust our actions** toward the standard we've set.

To close the gaps, we've got to know what they are!

This means measurement!

"Someone calling themselves
a customer says they want
something called service."

PRACTICAL TACTICS: (Questions to ponder)

What promises are you making? What expectations are you creating? Are you measuring operations performance and execution? Continuously? Of all customers? At each touchpoint?

The _actual_ customer experience:
The "missing link" in CRM and research

It's not just about who the customers <u>are</u>, or what they <u>like and dislike</u>. It's about what they are <u>experiencing</u>!

CRM is good, but...
CRM has been all the rage over the last 10–15 years. I've been around, purchased, and helped build some big ol' customer relationship management systems. But, my favorite CRM system is still the one that Ritz-Carlton had when I was on the team that acquired the luxury hotel chain for Marriott. It was not sophisticated, but it worked. Here's how: all employees had a small pad of cards in their pocket. When they noticed a customer like or dislike, they would write it down on the pad – things like, "the guest ate only the strawberries from the fruit plate," or "customer prefers late checkout," etc. At the end of the day, the cards were deposited into a shoe box, and then later entered into a spreadsheet. Fabulous! Way ahead of its time. This simple system put Ritz-Carlton on the map. Today, wonderfully sophisticated CRM systems are available. These systems tell us all about a customer's history and their likes and dislikes, but _they do not usually tell us if the customer got what they expected_ from their most recent experience.

Market research is good, but...
On the other hand, market research gives us a good feel for the _average_ customer experience. Through sampling techniques, a company extrapolates from what a few customers experience, to how the "average" customer generally feels. (We use market research to help clients understand the broad customer view and to assist with demographics and new product or service acceptance.) But market research is usually _not targeted toward improving operations_, but rather toward understanding customers.

Wouldn't you rather look forward?
The challenge with traditional customer-centric approaches like CRM and market research is that they: (1) are not _timely,_ and (2) only show a _partial view_ of the customer experience. Typically, CRM systems assist companies by collecting useful marketing and demographic data, rather than addressing existing customer needs. Market research is valuable in understanding product requirements and profiling potential customers, but is not usually set up to understand the needs of _tonight's_ customers. I've seen companies use CRM systems to track information as detailed as the customer's birth date, but then have no idea what the customer experienced only an hour ago when

they called the company's call center with an issue. I've seen restaurant chains use sophisticated market research to determine that their salsa is too mild in San Diego, but have no clue what an individual customer experienced in their restaurant today!

When I lived in Washington, DC, I occasionally used a transportation service that had detailed personal and historical information about me. They knew where to pick me up at the airport, they would recognize me, they had newspapers I liked, they knew my home address, and they knew which credit card I preferred. I thought their service was pretty darn smooth. Then one cold night they sent a new driver to the airport. He wanted to wait for additional passengers, which was fine with me. So, trying to gauge our departure time, I asked him the following question, "Should I wait inside or outside?" – (In essence, I was politely trying to ask, "when will we be leaving?") His answer, and I am not making this up, was, "*You look like a reasonably intelligent man. Why don't you decide?*" I wonder if the company even noticed that I never used them again. All the customer data in the world couldn't overcome such a poor experience.

Over the years, a number of well-thought-out approaches to managing and measuring customer service have been developed. (Some have already generated their own three-letter acronyms.) But to me, the most important part of measuring any customer experience can still be summed up in the simple question, **"How'd it go?"**

Customer experiences are created through multiple company touch points: advertising, retail service, call center agents, field service technicians, web sites, social media, etc. To retain customers, companies need to understand these various touch points and know what the customer is experiencing at each one. By inviting *each* customer to give feedback (not just a sampling, and not just a snapshot), a company is demonstrating its commitment to continuous service improvement. In my opinion, the best current vehicle for doing this is *the real-time customer survey.*

PRACTICAL TACTICS: (Questions to ponder)

Do you know how customers perceive you tonight? Do you have measurement tools in place to capture real-time customer feedback? Do you have processes in place to take action on that feedback?

Results: Why do this?

"What's in it for us?"

Boy, this is going to be a lot of work! Right? Not really. Most of it is common sense – it just seems like a lot to remember. So why would your company go through all of this effort? What's the payoff? Here are some persuasive reasons:

1. Make More Money

*Companies can boost profits by 25% to 85% by retaining just 5% more of their customers.** (Research with our clients has similarly shown strong correlations between increased satisfaction and increased sales.) How does this happen?

- Customers will become word-of-mouth *advocates*.
- You will gain more *up-selling* and *cross-selling* opportunities.
- Loyal customers are *more profitable*; among other things, they…
    - Buy more and return more often.
    - Tell their friends and bring in new customers.
    - Are less sensitive to price.
    - Are more protected from competitive threats.
    - Are more likely to forgive a problem.

Satisfying customers is a means to an end. With the appropriate management actions, satisfied employees can become loyal and productive employees, and satisfied customers can become loyal customers – and profits increase. An overly simplified diagram of the process looks like this:

A Service Profit Chain Model

Leadership	Commitment		Loyalty		Results
Management actions	Satisfied employees	Loyal and productive employees	Satisfied customers	Loyal customers	Increased Profits

(Adapted from "Putting the Service-Profit Chain to Work," by Heskett, et al, Harvard Business Review, March 1994)

(I strongly recommend that you read all of the publications listed in the back of this book on The Service Profit Chain concepts, by Heskett, et al.)

* (From "Zero Defections: Quality Comes to Services," by Frederick Reichheld and W. Earl Sasser, Jr., Harvard Business Review, Sept. 1990.)

> ## The "Bottom Line" is YOUR BOTTOM LINE
>
> *Operations Improvement through Customer Involvement*
> Drives
> *Increased Customer Satisfaction*
> Helps Drive
> *Increased Customer Loyalty*
> Drives
> *Increased Profits!*

2. Generate a Higher Stock Price*

Recent studies have conclusively shown that organizations that consistently deliver superior customer service are:

- More likely to enjoy *higher and more stable cash flows.*
- Able to consistently and significantly *outperform the stock market.*
- Deliver these *superior returns with lower risk.*

The summary in one scholarly study concluded with this declaration:

"Satisfied customers are economic assets with high returns and low risk."*

3. Minimize Risk

By understanding customer issues **as they occur**, companies are able to:

- Identify at-risk customers before they leave.
- Recover lost customers.
- Evaluate new products and services immediately.
- Gain better knowledge of weaknesses and strengths, so business decisions are objective, not subjective.

4. Improve Operations

Continuous customer involvement allows you to:

- Fix problem processes before they become ingrained.
- Pinpoint needed areas of training.
- Bring customer feedback from all collection sources together, and down to the level where the service is delivered.
- Improve manager efficiency.

* (From "Customer Satisfaction and Stock Prices," by Claes Fornell et al., Journal of Marketing, Jan 2006.)

- Develop standards based on customer needs and wants.
- Evaluate and rank employee performance.
- Recognize, publicize, and reward exemplary customer service.

5. Develop Closer Ties to Customers

Listening and responding to customer feedback allows:

- Customers to feel like their input really counts.
- Implementation of customer ideas that will develop trust (i.e., the customer will want to show friends "the suggestion I made").
- Companies have a finger on the pulse of customer trends. This is especially important as today's differentiators become tomorrow's "price-of-entry."

DEVELOPING LOYAL CUSTOMERS - PROTECT YOUR INVESTMENT

On average...*

- It costs 5–10 times as much to secure a new customer than to retain an existing customer.

- Upset customers will tell 8–10 other people about their bad experiences.**

- Customers who have their complaint resolved are up to 8% MORE loyal *than if they had never had a problem.*

ATTRACTING NEW CUSTOMERS

Direct Sales · Indirect Sales · Direct Marketing · Advertising · Promotions

your customer bucket

$

$

STOP LOSING EXISTING CUSTOMERS

* TARP Studies: 1986-1998

** But see next page for a discussion of Internet exposure.

To summarize the listed benefits:

- ☑ **More cash**
- ☑ **Higher profits**
- ☑ **Lower costs**
- ☑ **Higher stock price**
- ☑ **Stronger customer loyalty**
- ☑ **Insights to improve your business**
- ☑ **Overall effectiveness**

Common Sense Effort!
Common Sense Rewards!

Here is one final reason you must measure and improve:

THE INTERNET HAS CHANGED EVERYTHING.

Historically, upset customers would tell 8–10 other people about their bad experience. That was before the Internet. Now, in seconds, a disgruntled customer can tell millions of other people about your service lapse.

For example: One of the country's biggest home services companies sent a repair technician to the home of a customer. The repairman was kept on hold by his own support desk for an hour! While waiting, he fell asleep on the customer's couch. The angry customer got his camera, shot a video of the sleeping technician, and posted it on an Internet video-sharing site for all the world to see. As this book is being printed, that video has been viewed millions of times.

You can no longer afford unrecovered service lapses!

PRACTICAL TACTICS: (Questions to ponder)

Do you understand the return on investment from becoming a customer-centric organization? Do you believe? Are you prepared to shift to the longer-term mentality of customer loyalty in order to significantly increase future profits? Would you make the trade-off with short-term profits to accomplish this (if necessary)?

Focusing on the basics:
The importance of fundamentals

Avoid over-complicating simple things

It is always a temptation to make service measurement too complex.

If you have leanings toward the theoretical and the academic, it is fairly easy with this particular subject to find yourself sliding down the slippery slope of …

- Mental gymnastics about insignificant nuances.
- Masterful analytics of accurate but unusable information.
- Incredibly precise measurements of "milking mice."

In defense of most of the wonderful authors, consultants, and academics I've studied, it is not that I find their research incorrect or without incredible merit, but rather that I find most of their conclusions "beyond the mark" of most service businesses who are "living the everyday." To use a football analogy, a coach might develop a brilliantly sophisticated offensive play, but without months and months of proper conditioning and basic blocking and execution skills by the offensive line, the quarterback will never get a chance to implement it – he'll be flat on his back.

> **It is fairly easy with this particular subject to find yourself sliding down the slippery slope of mental gymnastics about insignificant nuances, masterful analytics of accurate but unusable information, and incredibly precise measurements of "milking mice."**

Deep analytical research can be mentally stimulating and may even provide your company with a unique edge in specific areas, but it isn't generally where the "low-hanging fruit" exists. Almost always, the 80/20 rule points to *basic execution* as the first place to focus.

However, for the sake of completeness, let me mention some academic complexities that you might want to explore in more depth in a year (or two or three) – <u>after</u> you master the basics.

1. Customer loyalty vs. customer satisfaction

Here's the first example: Did you know that customer *satisfaction* and customer *loyalty* are not the same? In fact, some research studies have shown that more than half of lost customers reported being "very satisfied," or "satisfied," just prior to defecting. There are some wonderful academic studies outlining the differences between loyalty and satisfaction. It is now generally accepted that loyalty is a higher-order commitment than satisfaction, and that loyalty involves invoking some sort of *emotional attachment* from the customer. It is also true that customers can be satisfied, but not committed or not loyal, and therefore will not return. The academics love to debate this kind of thing. Some will define loyalty as an *attitude,* others will say loyalty is only about *behavior.*

All good stuff. Clever and thought provoking. And very important (see the next chapter, titled "Loyalty: wallet, mind, and mouth").

But it's also true that *one horrific service experience* can cause a customer to never even give the emotional attachment of loyalty a second subconscious thought. For example, if the restrooms are filthy dirty in your establishment, it doesn't matter how emotionally attached a customer has become to your company, you may never see them again.

2. Gaps in "recommending" and "referring"

In measuring loyalty, two specific gaps should not be overlooked: (1) the gap between what customers say they'll do, and what they actually do, and (2) the gap between those who spend the most money with you versus those who generate the most revenue for you.

(1) Some practitioners of customer satisfaction research will call attention to a gap that sometimes exists between those who *say* they are "highly likely to recommend" your company and those who actually end up recommending you. (2) They also occasionally present data showing that those who are most loyal (as measured by the amount of business they give you), are not necessarily the most valuable to your business because they are unwilling to become advocates and will not refer you to others. They point out that those who are the most loyal to your company sometimes make you less money than someone who actually buys less from you, but who *refers* a lot of business to you.

These are two important concepts to investigate. And again, there are sure to be multiple consultants and consulting firms happy to perform the fairly sophisticated and time-consuming pre- and post-purchase research necessary to investigate such behaviors. Once again, however, even such fascinating and useful information takes a back seat to *executing* against established operational standards in the short run.

3. Chasing the wrong customers

The basic premise of this nuance of customer research is that you might be perfectly serving a customer that you would be better off "firing." For example, if a customer only buys low-margin products from you, it may cost your company more to serve them than the revenue they generate. Understanding the profitability of individual customers or customer segments is something I strongly encourage you to do, but it too is beyond the scope of this book.

Back to the basics

Here's the point: There is some sophisticated and interesting research one can do, but like many of you, after years of exploring the deep and academic nuances of customer service, I'm even more convinced that *the biggest wins come in executing the basics.* J. Willard Marriott and Conrad Hilton expressed this concept better than I could. Here's what they are quoted as having summarized:

"Hot food HOT, Cold food COLD!"

(J. W. Marriott)

"Leave the shower curtain on the inside of the tub!"

(Conrad Hilton)

So sure, read the books, go to the seminars, and attend the one-week executive education programs. But, when you've finished delving into the mysteries of the academic...come back to reality and *focus on the fundamentals.*

Remember, if it's not simple, no one will use it!

Measuring five basic things

I've found that the service experience generally involves the measurement and improvement of **five basic customer experience areas:**

1. The *product or service* they came to buy.
2. The *person or team* that delivered it.
3. The *process* of doing business with your organization.
4. The *atmosphere, location,* or *method* that encompassed it.
5. The *confidence* and *reassurance* they've felt during their experience.

I suggest you focus on these five areas.

Here's what Baron Rothschild is quoted as having said about his desired hotel experience:

> **"I want my bath to run hot in two minutes flat. I don't want to hear plumbing noises. I want a good bed and pillows. I want my breakfast right away. I want good croissants. I want people to be polite to me, and I don't want to hear their side of the story."**

The truth is that concentrating on the basics can be rather boring. It's focus. It's details. It's sometimes drudgery. It's repetition and consistency – but that's why it's the "big win." It's not really all that hard. For example, a simple smile and "thank you" can change a customer's day.

Very few people want to focus on what I call the "boring everyday," ...

... but ...

... it's the "boring everyday" that will make you stand out.

PRACTICAL TACTICS: (Questions to ponder)
What are your top customer compliments and complaints? List and categorize. If "other" is too big, break it down further. What do they absolutely love about you? Where are you falling short? Are you excelling at the "core delivery" of your company? Does your training focus on the "blocking and tackling" of service in your industry?

Loyalty: wallet, mind, and mouth

It's all for naught if they don't come back

What is loyalty? Why is it so important? How does it differ from satisfaction? Does this matter?

Welcome to one of *the* most hotly debated issues in all of customer research. In the spirit of the common sense approach of this guidebook, let me try and summarize this for you.

Customer loyalty defined

Loyalty is a higher-order measure of customer attachment than satisfaction. Loyalty involves an *emotional commitment* or tie to your brand. It usually has an *attitude* component ("I <u>feel</u> better about it, so I'll keep using it") and a *behavior* component ("I'm going to keep buying it"). Attitudes are important because buying again doesn't always mean a customer is "emotionally invested." For example, you may not like your insurance agent, but you renew with him each year because you don't have the time to look for a new one. Then your friend tells you about a new agent and you switch. You weren't really loyal to the first agent all those years, you were just opting for the convenient solution.

Customers demonstrate true loyalty when they have to choose between options. You don't want customers to continue buying from you simply because they have no other choice or they are locked into a contract. When a customer chooses to be loyal to a brand or service, he is less likely to defect and more likely to buy again, think about you first, and refer you to others. That's why I like the definition of customer loyalty as a **higher share of wallet, mind, and mouth.**

But what of satisfaction?

Generally, most loyal customers are very satisfied, but not all satisfied customers are loyal. They may be satisfied with you, but with the slightest irritation, off they go to talk to your competitor. On the other hand, customer satisfaction plays a key role in retaining customers and driving them toward loyalty (i.e., if your operations are horrific, customers will never get to the point where emotion and attitude transform their satisfaction into loyalty).

Measuring loyalty

What is the best measure of loyalty? Short answer: there isn't one single best measure. Each industry, each situation is different – and regardless of how appealing a single metric might be, it just isn't possible for one size to fit all (see the chapter entitled "Take no shortcuts," page 35). Some research studies point to "likelihood to recommend" as the best measure of loyalty. Other research points to "overall satisfaction" as the metric most correlated to future profits. Still others use a "behavior probability" method that has customers allocate points (e.g., "of the next ten times you eat at a casual restaurant, how many of those ten visits will be at *this* restaurant?"). It would appear that each consultant has his or her own "right way" to measure loyalty.

The truth is this: the best measure of customer loyalty for your business is the one that leads to ***long-term, repeat buying behavior and referrals*** from your customers, and therefore ***more profits*** for you. However, teasing this out of the data can be a complex and time-consuming process. Until there is enough data to establish a relationship between "best predictive" customer metric(s) and profits, I recommend a three-question composite index comprised of "overall satisfaction," "likelihood to repurchase," and "likelihood to recommend" as a proxy for loyalty. This is sometimes called the customer satisfaction index (CSI) or the customer loyalty index (CLI), and has been used for years.

Once a loyalty metric (or its proxy) has been chosen, it is then used as the dependent variable against which individual service issues are statistically measured in order to derive those service issues (key drivers) that have the greatest impact on customer satisfaction and loyalty.

What should I aim for?

Your end goal should be generating loyal customers. (There are lots of books and plenty of consultants itching to sell you "their special sauce" to help you transform satisfied customers into loyal ones.) But I believe good old customer satisfaction should not be left on the side of the road, sacrificed to the enticements of the goal of loyalty. Why? Because, as I mentioned in the Introduction, my experience has led me to conclude that **significantly more companies are failing due to poor execution than are failing due to poor strategy** (including a zealous attachment to over-analyzing loyalty).

For example, let's say that in a seafood restaurant, the most loyal of all customers bites into a piece of greasy, under-cooked fish – suddenly her loyalty evaporates. Larry Loyalty phones a reservations call center to book his next hotel room and is treated so rudely that he never calls again. And, after getting your haircut at the same place for 12 years, you finally can't take the excruciating wait any longer, so you go to a salon down the street.

Each of these real-life examples illustrates why I wrote this book – because I believe a concerted focus on executing the basics is the single most important thing your business can do today. In simple terms, I think there is more bang for the buck in stopping customers from leaving you in the first place, than in spending your life trying to make them fit some definition of loyalty.

There is also more money to be made in customer retention than in new customer acquisition. I love this quote:

> ## "American business has developed an insane imbalance between *customer acquisition* and *customer retention*. Many companies will invest millions in sales and marketing costs to bring customers in the door and then throw a few thousand dollars at trying to keep them."*

That was written in 1992 and is still valid today!

That's why the focus of this book is on *real-time feedback, leading to local accountability, and continuously focusing on improving operations* – so that you can keep customers coming back long enough to allow them to become emotionally involved – *to become loyal!*

PRACTICAL TACTICS: (Questions to ponder)

Do you understand the importance of loyal customers to your business? Do you understand "share-of-wallet" and other metrics that can serve as proxy for measuring that kind of customer loyalty? Do you agree that a focus on fundamentals and execution will give you the biggest bang for your service buck?

---

* *(From "Firing On All Cylinders: The Service/Quality System for High-Powered Corporate Performance," by Jim Clemmer, TCG Press, Apr 1992.)*

How strong is your resolve?

There is no "quit" in a winner

- Delivering great customer service is a business requirement – you have no choice if you want to win!

- Measuring customer satisfaction is not a fad – it needs to become an integral part of how you do business, day in and day out!

Some essential questions you need to be able to answer:

- Do you truly believe in the two statements above?

- If you are a multi-unit operator, 10% to 15% of your managers (or franchisees) may attempt to sabotage any measurement system that they can't control. Are you prepared to persist anyway, because you know this is the right thing to do?

- Can your employees accept honest feedback without taking it personally?

- It may take you some time to see results! Do you have the resolve and staying power to hold on until the results begin to materialize? (See cartoon.)

- Is your company willing to take an openly critical look at its weaknesses, with the end goal of becoming stronger?

- Holding people accountable may make you unpopular. Do you have the determination and stamina to fight off objections thrown in your path?

"And here is the uptrend I promised you!"

- One oft-quoted definition of insanity is: "Doing the same thing over and over again, but expecting different results."* Is your company willing to *make the changes* that may be required to succeed with your customers?

* (Variously attributed to Albert Einstein, Benjamin Franklin, and Rita Mae Brown.)

Strength in Tenacity

Part II

Cultural Catalysts of Service

It's about customers, not you!

The Platinum Rule of Customer Service

Years ago I attended a seminar where Dr. Tony Alessandra introduced the audience to the concept of the **Platinum Rule.*** Most of us are familiar with the **Golden Rule** and strive to live by it:

"Do unto others as _you_ would have them do unto _you_."

"Treat others how you want to be treated" has been endorsed by all the great world religions. Jesus and Confucius each used it to summarize their ethical teachings. The Golden Rule teaches consistency and fairness between people.

That day, Dr. Alessandra introduced us to the **Platinum Rule**:

"Do unto others as _they_ would have you do unto _them_."

The Platinum Rule builds on the Golden Rule by recognizing that we have very different preferences than those around us. Said more simply: **people may not like what you like – give them what _they_ like, not what _you_ like.**

There are opportunities all around for companies to mess up on the Platinum Rule. You go to a stylist to get your hair cut. She loves conversation and assumes you do too. But you prefer to be left alone with your thoughts. Then there is the old story of the Boy Scout who assisted the elderly lady across the street, only to discover that she didn't want to cross the street.

An important part of the Platinum Rule is to find out what customers want **before** we start creating the solution. (I've always loved the old joke about the software manager who says to his colleague, "You get started coding and I'll find out what they want.")

My exposure to the Platinum Rule has come by watching truly great service companies capitalize on it by providing extraordinary experiences for their customers. This simple concept can make all the difference in the way a service provider designs and executes its product and service offerings. The focus

* (The Platinum Rule is a trademark of Dr. Tony Alessandra - http://www.platinumrule.com.)

shifts from, "this is what I want, so I'll give it to everyone," to "first I need to understand what customers want, and then I'll give it to them." The key is to listen and observe what a customer needs or appreciates and then try to satisfy those needs.

Alfred B. Sloan, Former Chairman of General Motors said it best:

"The quickest way to profits... is to serve the customer *in ways in which the customer* wants to be served."*

At Mindshare, we provide automated customer feedback across more than 25 service industries, which gives us a front-row seat to a wide range of customers' perceptions of service. For example, let's go back to the case of what I call "Chatty Cathy" in the salon industry. Many people go to the barbershop or salon for two main reasons: (1) get a haircut, and (2) engage in pleasant conversation with a stylist. A talkative, chatting stylist fits this need exactly. But some of us just want to be left alone. A haircut is a time of thoughtful contemplation about…well, nothing. How do the truly great salon companies use this to their advantage? They note the customer's preference each time they visit, and then meet those expectations. Some even go so far as to ask the customer, "Do you feel like talking today?"

> The **Golden Rule** of Loving Our Neighbors:
> ### Do unto others as _you_ would have done unto _you_.
>
> The **Platinum Rule** of Customer Service:
> ### Do unto others as _they_ would have done unto _them_!

A fabulous Chinese restaurant I visit asks the following question as the patrons are seated, "Would you like me to leave a pitcher of water on the table, or would you prefer I fill your glasses throughout the evening?"

Common sense stuff.

(From a letter to General Motors stockholders, Sept. 1933.)

I went to a restaurant that understands and implements the Platinum Rule. I ordered a meal that came with beets as the included vegetable. Not being a big fan of beets, I asked if I could trade them in for boiled potatoes. "Absolutely. No problem at all," came the reply.

Contrast that to an earlier experience at a different restaurant. Same issue, but without the beets. When I asked to trade an item, the server said that no substitutions were allowed. I tried again, and got the infamous answer, "Sorry, company policy."

Speaker Shep Hyken had a similar experience with restaurants and commented on what a big mistake management is making when they do things like this. He said,

> **"You've surely heard of 'Total Customer Satisfaction?' Well welcome to 'Partial Customer Satisfaction,' where a business gets (only) a percentage of the business they could."***

"Sorry, company policy" is not a great recipe for success, is it?

The practical application of The Platinum Rule of Customer Service is fairly simple:

1. **Ask customers what they want.**
2. **Figure out how to deliver it.**
3. **Monitor to make sure you're consistently delivering** (i.e., continuously administer real-time customer surveys).
4. **Change as needed to improve your operations** (e.g., immediate training or process changes).
5. **Make sure employees are continuously involved in steps 1-4.**

PRACTICAL TACTICS: (Questions to ponder)
Are you delivering what your customers want, or what you **_think_** they want? How do you know the difference? Have you asked them?

---

* *(Shep Hyken, "The Cult of the Customer," www.hyken.com.)*

Service: attitude, process, and skills

Hiring attitude, training process, teaching skills

In the late 1980's and early 1990's a wave of *Total Quality Management* (TQM) swept the United States. Businesses latched on to TQM and W. Edwards Demming finally got recognized in the United States. (Decades earlier he had helped transform "Made in Japan" from a negative slogan to a positive one by evangelizing TQM in Japan – hence Toyota, Sony, etc.) TQM is a participative management style that stresses staff commitment to total customer satisfaction. TQM achieves its objective through data collection, flow charts, cause-and-effect diagrams, and other analytical tools that expose problems and flaws in a company's processes. A principle concept of TQM is removing *process variation.*

I was a big proponent of TQM. I still am. Those of you who love process techniques will love TQM. But, over time, I've come to believe that it isn't enough to fix processes. First, you've got to fix employee attitudes.

"Go tell the workers that I'm serious about this quality crap."

I call it the "plays well with others" trait. I remember working with someone early in my career who was an absolute genius, but simply could not get along with anyone. Even more challenging was the fact that she was not teachable and unable to accept criticism in any form. Most people thought she was a jerk. In the "good old days" a company might have been able to hide such an employee's attitude. But in today's real-time, camera-phone, social media, Internet world, companies full of jerky employees on the inside, soon get reputations of being jerky companies in the marketplace.

One of the most important required employee attitudes is the ability to deal with complaints.

Have you read the book, *A Complaint is a Gift*, by Barlow and Møller? I believe this book is one of the seminal works of customer satisfaction. (Its title alone makes it worth buying.) Let me paraphrase a few of the book's most relevant concepts:

> One of the most meaningful ways customers can express their dissatisfaction to companies is through **a complaint.** In order for us to treat complaints as gifts, we need to achieve a complete shift in perception and attitude about the role of complaints in our relationships. This requires separating the message of the complaint from the emotion of being blamed.
>
> Rather than falling prey to the seductive allure of *complaint reduction,* we need to talk about *complaint management* or handling. (If a company's goal is to have fewer complaints, it is a very easy goal to accomplish. *Staff will get the message and simply stop reporting complaints to management.* How many times have you delivered a written complaint to a business, and wondered if the complaint got *passed on to supervisors*?) Sir Colin Marshall talks about the way things were at British Airways: "We used to ignore complaints. We tried to make it difficult for the complainant by insisting telephone callers write in, and by adhering strictly to a rule book that allowed us to tell customers that they were at fault by breaking a BA regulation which they weren't even aware of." *

The key is to help employees understand that complaints are an incredible source of improvement information. Research has found that if companies can get customers to complain directly to them, they can minimize the damage. Customers who complain are *also more likely to repurchase*, even if their complaint is not handled satisfactorily. In fact, the research concluded that *customers who do not complain are the least loyal customers*. Those who complain may become the *most loyal customers.*

---

* *(Reprinted with permission. From "A Complaint is a Gift," 1996 by Janelle Barlow and Claus Møller, Berrett-Koehler Publishers Inc., All rights reserved.)*

The practical application is for senior management to:

1. *Cultivate an environment* where a complaint is treated as a gift, and
2. *Hire and train employees* who will operationalize that philosophy.

Basketball coaches know the simple maxim, "You can't teach height." Likewise, you can't teach attitude, you need to *hire it*. Experienced managers understand that service attitude begins with *correct hiring*.

Here's the best kept secret about hiring:

"Hire based on a person's *attitude*, teach them *skills* later."

If you rely on training to change someone's attitude, you'll be disappointed, because so-called "smile training" usually just produces "cheerful incompetents." The bottom line? Hire for attitude and teachability. Get the right people, then fix the processes. (You can teach them skills later.)

Remember, service involves <u>attitude</u>, <u>process,</u> and <u>skills</u>!

"I hope you're not one
of our stupid customers
demanding better service."

PRACTICAL TACTICS: (Questions to ponder)

How are complaints viewed by your front-line employees? Do they have incentive to "hide" them from senior management? Do you currently hire for skills or for attitude?

Time in the trenches

The bigger a company gets, the further its executives get from its products and services

Executives sometimes get so far removed from what their company actually does that they can't speak authentically about their company's strengths and weaknesses. To combat that, when I worked in the hotel business, I encouraged all of my employees (from Senior VPs on down) to work in a hotel at least one week each year. We called this "cleaning the toilets." (By the way, not only is this a good strategy for connecting corporate employees with the field, but it's actually fun for most people and keeps them in touch with the company's "bread and butter" business.)

"Our bureaucracy is so vast, we no longer need reality."

It is amazing to me how many people have "graduated" from doing actual work. From the executive who feels it is "beneath" him to make photocopies, to the call center manager who refuses to "mystery shop" or "ghost" actual customer calls, to the senior restaurant executive I spoke with recently who hadn't visited a store in eight months.

Contrast this with the attitude of Howard Schultz, the founder of Starbucks, who I am told, still visits 25 stores a week. Another great example is Bill Marriott. When I worked for Mr. Marriott, he was still visiting 200+ hotels a year. (By the way, no matter how quiet we tried to keep his visits, inevitably someone at the hotel would find out and get things spic and span. In fact, there was an ongoing joke we used to tell – "We enjoy making hotel property visits with Mr. Marriott, because we love the smell of Brasso and fresh paint.") The point is that great leaders like Schultz and Marriott stay close to their operations.

At Mindshare, every employee is involved with our clients. When we first started the company, every employee took customer service calls. Because we collect a huge amount of automated telephone surveys each day, many of the customer support calls were from an older segment of the population who were trying to take a survey, and "couldn't get the darn phone to work." (I actually looked forward to hearing from these sweet people, many of whom would talk for hours and hours.)

The other day, I ordered at the drive-thru of a well-known fast-food restaurant. The window was dirty, the bricks outside were worn. The back of the cash register (facing me) was grimy and quite possibly incubating a "science experiment." I thought to myself, "I bet they don't know this is such a lousy experience from the customer's viewpoint." Things appeared to be spotless inside the restaurant, but outside it was a miserable experience. I wonder how long it's been since anyone in management has experienced the drive-thru as seen *through the customer's eyes.*

> *"No good decision was ever made in a swivel chair."*

Here's the summary: For one week, why not get away from your desk and *experience what the customer experiences…*on your front lines! Go wash a dish or two, take a couple of phone calls, flip a burger, sell a dress, take an order, or try to calm down an irate customer. After trying this, you may agree with a statement attributed to General George S. Patton, "No good decision was ever made in a swivel chair."

PRACTICAL TACTICS: (Questions to ponder)

When was the last time you worked on the front line? When was the last time you experienced your company's service anonymously? When was the last time you slept in your company's beds, or ordered your product online, or tasted your food, or had a haircut, or took a customer service call, etc.?

Dealing with mistakes

Enhancing employee self-confidence by tolerating failure
(But not all the time)

Here are a couple of my favorite quotes on this subject:

"Mistakes are the portals of discovery."
(James Joyce)

"I have not failed; I've just found ten thousand ways that won't work."
(Thomas Edison)

Great customer-centric service companies allow employees to make mistakes. In fact, a number of organizations (including companies, non-profits, sports teams, and families) attribute much of their success to accepting and learning from mistakes. They focus less on the person who made the mistake, and more on learning from what went wrong. Creativity and great service seem to thrive. Sadly, the opposite is also true. There are organizations where fear of making a mistake has caused them to become stagnant, almost paralyzed. One frequent example of this occurs in athletics when a team builds a lead in a game, but then loses momentum because players start to fear that they will make the big mistake that might "cost the game."

One of the problems of intolerance toward mistakes is that it keeps them from being corrected quickly when they happen. In companies where mistakes are not allowed, people stop focusing on moving forward and get side-tracked on covering up mistakes. This can lead to employees trying to protect themselves and wasting time trying to hide mistakes. (Think of all the lost energy over the years spent in "mistake concealment" by government officials.)

So, if tolerating mistakes can be so beneficial, why don't organizations tolerate them and why are individuals so afraid of making them?

The Answer?   Ego!   Pride!   Fear!

Tolerating Some Failure

The ability to truly check one's ego and do what is right for the organization says a lot about a person's self-confidence. The most confident leaders I know are also the most teachable and quickly admit their mistakes. They teach others by their example.

Dale Carnegie is quoted as having said:

"If you lay an egg, step back and admire it."

If you want your company to lead in customer service, you need to make it safe for employees to risk making a mistake. Of course, you don't need to accept someone making the same mistakes over and over again – this can be just as bad as not tolerating mistakes. But by allowing for mistakes as a normal course of business, you will be taking one of the steps needed to become a truly great customer-centric organization!

Here are a few ideas to help make an organization more accepting of mistakes, and therefore, more risk-tolerant:

- Create an award for the best mistake of the quarter.
- Senior executives should be willing to admit their own mistakes.
- Don't dwell on mistakes or who made them. Instead, talk about what was learned and focus on the future.
- Make sure your private and public methods for dealing with mistakes are the same.
- Make anonymous and frequent employee satisfaction surveys a part of your culture.
- Teach employees about great leaders whose eventual success followed multiple previous failures.
- Base bonuses on learning from mistakes (improvement), rather than just absolute scores.

PRACTICAL TACTICS: (Questions to ponder)
Is your company tolerant of mistakes? How do you know? Would your employees agree with you? Are your most senior leaders willing to admit their mistakes?

Becoming the customer champion

Commit to customer feedback, and even better, <u>you</u> become the champion!

Do you want to climb the company ladder? Unless you are the chairman of your company's board of directors, I have some career advice for you:

MAKE DECISIONS!   DECIDE TO DECIDE!   HAVE A SPINE!

You see, companies have no conscience, companies make no decisions. It is individual *employees* that make the difference. It is individual *champions* that make the difference. Another favorite poem…

"Stroll every park, search every city, you'll find no monument to a committee."*

A lot of people in business just try to survive another day. They hide behind meetings and teams and groups and try to keep their head low. This disease has been prevalent in every big company I've worked for – its root cause is fear, and its main symptom is paralysis in making a decision. Granted, some decisions need a wider buy-in, but not every decision. In fact, I'd argue that most businesses grind to a halt because of the "cover yer butt" mentality of many mid-level managers. These are the folks who try to make sure they've gotten 100% consensus from all involved before deciding anything. Contrast that attitude with one taught by Steve Weisz, one of my mentors:

"Consensus is rare. In any organization, when you try to reach the lowest common denominator, you are assured of <u>mediocrity</u>. You just can't make everyone happy. You have to make the tough decisions."

(Stephen P. Weisz)

* *(Anonymous. A similar quote has been attributed to Victoria Pasternak.)*

Becoming the Champion!

Have you seen the de-motivator posters at **www.despair.com?** Here's the text of my favorite one…it describes how I feel about "group think," and most meetings:

MEETINGS
None of us is as dumb as all of us.

You're not one of those people are you? You want to make a difference, right? Then **become the champion** in your company for customer service and customer experience measurement! Take a risk. Lay it out there. Commit yourself and your company to becoming truly customer-centric. Demonstrate that it's a part of the fabric of your company. I promise you…you can make the difference.

Here's the simple summary of this important point:

"Our task, then, is to decide how to decide how to decide."

"Every institution is merely the lengthened shadow of an individual."

(Ralph Waldo Emerson)

You be that individual champion who makes the difference. *You be* the customer-centric guru of your company! Act like the chief customer officer! Get involved!

PRACTICAL TACTICS: (Questions to ponder)

Who is making decisions? Are you? Or, are you a drone, a robot? Customer-centricity is not the "default" position of companies; it will require a CHAMPION to drive it! Are you that champion?

Take no shortcuts

No shortcuts in customer service or in measurement
(They <u>will</u> notice – They <u>will</u> mind)

"Go ahead and nail it; we'll caulk it later." This gem of wisdom was presented to me in 1976, when, as a 16 year-old young man, I was dangling on scaffolding working above two carpenters on my parents' new home. The carpenters evidently had forgotten that I was there. They were finishing up the installation of some paneling below me. One man was fitting the final piece and had mistakenly measured it short. Following his discovery, he said a few words I hadn't heard before, and then he questioned the other man about what to do. The older carpenter replied, "Go ahead and nail it; we'll caulk it later." To which the younger man responded, "Yeah, it's good enough for who it's for." (Mom and Dad weren't all that excited when I reported this conversation to them.)

That story brings to mind this quote:

"'Good enough' never is."*

Here's some advice: whatever it is, do it right the first time. Don't skimp on raw materials. Don't squeeze super-human productivity out of over-worked employees. Even if it costs a little bit more, do it right. Eventually, all attempts at taking shortcuts come back around and bite you. Then you're stuck with the additional costs of rework and remedying the situation.

My favorite tale on this subject is titled, "Cookies and incremental degradation." (I have no way to confirm its veracity, but the lesson is a good one.) Each year, a brand new crop of marketing MBAs would land on the "XYZ Cookies" brand team. Hoping to "make their mark," they would start fiddling with the cookie, a proven product. One year, a particularly bright fellow discovered (through research) that if they replaced some of the white creamy filling in the cookie with a lower cost raw product, they could save money, and (according to research) the customer wouldn't notice the difference. Accordingly, the change (toward the cheaper product) was made that year, and then year after year, with market research showing that the customer couldn't tell the difference between "before" and "after" formulations each year. Raw costs declined year after year. But eventually, sales began to fall. For years they struggled. Finally, another particularly

* *(Anonymous. Popularized by Debbi Fields.)*

bright fellow decided that instead of testing year (x) against year (x-1), he'd compare year (x) against the original formulation (before anyone had messed with the recipe). You've already guessed the outcome. While customers weren't noticing the year-over-year changes, they had obviously noticed the cumulative changes, and they had gradually stopped buying the cookies. The formulation was immediately changed back to the original, sales jumped back up, and everyone lived (and ate cookies) happily ever after.

This is similar to the instructions I've read on "how to boil a frog." Put him in a pot of boiling water, and he'll jump right out. But put him in a pot of lukewarm water, and slowly raise the temperature, and he'll be delicious.

Don't be a boiled frog. Do things right. Don't be cheap.

Getting lost in measurement shortcuts

By the way, "no shortcuts" also applies to measurement techniques. Some pundits have recently attempted to support the assertion that all customer experience monitoring can be simplified down to one single question – "How likely is it that you would **recommend** XYZ to a friend or colleague?" (This is akin to telling a doctor you feel ill, having him ask you "why?" and then allowing him no further questions.) There is a lot to be said about the simplicity of asking just one question - and, sometimes it increases survey response rates. But, common sense tells us that a single-question methodology cannot possibly be robust enough to provide the actionable information required to improve! Also, by discarding data, we are unable to evaluate the *details* of the answers. For example, how many "satisfied" customers are there? How many "very poor" experiences are there? Additionally, many customers are loyal and happy, but still not willing to recommend anything to anyone, so looking at just that one question can sometimes be misleading.

Rallying the company around a single measurement metric is a wonderful idea. Obviously, the best metric to use is the one that will lead to the greatest future profits for your specific company. (See chapter on "Loyalty: wallet, mind, and mouth," page 17.) However, while a single metric may be a very good ***goal*** and ***rallying point*** for a company, it provides no diagnostics about what ***actions*** to take to improve.

Surely the allure and simplicity of asking only a single question to determine customer satisfaction is appealing. On the surface, it sounds so inviting. It did to us at Mindshare. But when we tried to use a single question survey for many of our clients, we discovered its major utility flaw: **a lack of *actionable* information that our clients can actually use to improve their business.**

So, while I strongly believe in asking participants the "likelihood to recommend" question, I also suggest that my clients collect enough detailed information to highlight needed areas of improvement. This can be accomplished through automated text analytics, manual coding of customer voice recordings on open-ended questions, or by simply asking the customer enough targeted questions on the survey to provide actionable information.

H.L. Mencken had it right when he said:

"For every complex problem there is an answer that is clear, simple, and <u>wrong</u>."

"I'll just pile you up with the other customers. Someone will be able to assist you shortly."

So, here's the summary:
Don't skimp on service. Don't skimp on quality. Don't skimp on staffing.

And, when you measure the customer experience, don't be lured into skimping on what you need to know. Strongly avoid the temptation to take these shortcuts:

- 🚫 Sampling only
- 🚫 One-question techniques
- 🚫 Turn on, turn-off surveying
- 🚫 Annual studies in lieu of ongoing feedback
- 🚫 And any other similar trends or shortcuts

My simple belief is this: Shortcuts backfire. Always!

PRACTICAL TACTICS: (Questions to ponder)
(1) Where are you being tempted to take shortcuts in your service? Have you caught yourself saying something like, "It's okay, the customer won't notice?" (Guess what, they will.) Never skimp on service and quality.
(2) Are you being tempted to use one of the latest shortcut trends in measuring customer service? Ask yourself this, *"Will I be gathering 'actionable' information, about each of my employees, on a consistent basis?"*

Part III

Gathering Customer Experience Feedback

Performance measurement methods
"In God we trust, all others bring data"

(If you don't measure it, you can't improve it)

You've probably heard this wise old proverb:

"That which gets measured gets done."
(Anonymous)

I learned early in my career that if you don't set expectations and then measure results, you'll only get mediocre performance in return.

How to measure
When it comes to measuring how well your employees are performing, there are multiple tools at your disposal. There are numerous efficiency and effectiveness measures. They include so-called *"hard"* measurements, such as units sold, hours worked, customers talked to, complaints resolved, etc.

Then, there are the more *subjective* metrics used to measure how well an employee is performing. At Mindshare, we work with major global companies in multiple industries. While the industries vary greatly, the general methods used to evaluate employees are easily grouped into a couple of buckets. Most types of performance measurement fall into one of three general areas: (1) internal quality auditing, (2) external mystery shopping, or (3) the actual customer experience. Let me briefly address each of these methods and their strengths and shortcomings.

Internal quality auditing
In call centers, this is usually called "ghosting" or "whispering." In food and retail locations, this is often called something like "supervisor shopping," "quality checks," or "internal shopping." With this method, employees of the company use their skills to *audit* a location and/or employees for adherence to processes and procedures.

> **Pros:** Company and policy knowledge, relatively inexpensive.
> **Cons:** Subjective and biased, ***not** the actual customer*, not continuous.

External mystery shopping

This is often called "mystery shopping," as conducted by "secret shoppers." In this method, *third parties* are paid to pretend they are a customer. They visit a location and perform detailed reviews of performance against pre-determined standards and specifications.

> **Pros**: Detailed, more areas can be graded, can measure processes.
>
> **Cons**: Questionable quality (because shoppers are not always sufficiently trained), expensive, ***not*** *the actual customer*, very small sample, not continuous, day-to-day inconsistencies will not get noticed.

Customer experience feedback

Sometimes called "customer satisfaction measurement," "compliance monitoring," or simply "customer feedback." In this method, *customers themselves* voluntarily leave comments about the experience they just had. Sometimes these are supplemented with active solicitation.

> **Pros**: Feedback from *the **actual customer***, anonymous, inexpensive, continuous, large sample.
>
> **Cons**: Not as precise in measuring compliance to desired processes.

Because Mindshare has its roots in mystery shopping, and our executives have significant experience in all three methods, I feel confident in my conclusion that, of the three methods, the most important is knowing what *the actual customer* perceived their service experience to be. A few clients use all three measurement tools to get a three-legged stool approach to measuring the service experience. However, the majority have migrated toward using only automated customer feedback surveys in lieu of any other performance measurement tool. If a client does choose to use two or three different types of feedback, they will often create an ***integrated dashboard*** of service measurement. For example, we have clients for whom we provide consolidated reporting, showing results from: (1) customer surveys, (2) internal quality or compliance audits, and (3) external mystery shops, in a single set of actionable reports. (See the chapter "EFM: bringing it all together," page 69, for a further discussion of integrated reporting.)

Next Steps (OK, I believe; now how do I get started?)

I almost titled this next section:

"We are trained professionals; do not try this at home."

Without question, this all looks much simpler than it really is. After all, aren't we just talking about surveys here? Why not use one of those cheap survey companies on the web? Another thing I occasionally hear is, "Let's just let the local unit managers choose for themselves, whether or not they want to participate in using a customer feedback tool." Allow me to hop up on my soapbox and present four very direct, very strongly-opinionated suggestions to you:

1. **HIRE PROFESSIONALS!** Do not let your IT department talk you into trying to build your own customer feedback system. (Remember, engineers love to make things.) There is a tendency to significantly underestimate both the complexity and cost of gathering and evaluating customer feedback. In any accurate "build vs. buy" analysis (which must include fully-loaded internal costs), it almost never makes economic sense to build your own system. Do you make your own electricity? Accounting software? POS systems? Etc. Of course not – these are not "what you do." Customer feedback measurement is not your core competency either. But it is the core competency of an expert vendor-partner.

   A homegrown system will never achieve the scale and cost leverage of a specialized vendor. For example, at Mindshare, we've spent seven years and millions and millions of dollars creating our purpose-built survey and reporting software, and developing comprehensive domain expertise. We collect information across hundreds of clients. That leverage means not only cheaper costs, but also significantly better features, more reliability, and a sharing of ideas and innovations across 25 industries. You also get the benefits of benchmarking against peer companies and sharing of best practices. But, perhaps the most important reason for using experts is the opportunity cost of taking your eye off your own core competency. The time and resources you spend trying to create your own feedback system should be focused elsewhere on *improving* your core business.

2. **START NOW!** The sooner you start collecting customer information, the sooner you will be able to establish objective norms and trends as a baseline. You need to get going on data collection right away. Even if you start today, you won't be able to look at seasonally-adjusted, year-over-year growth charts for at least 12 months! *Get started!*

3. **MAKE IT MANDATORY!** Lots of franchise organizations do a "slow voluntary roll-out" by allowing franchisees to choose if customer feedback is something they'd like to do. Think about this. Do you know anyone who *wants* to be measured and who will jump up and down with joy saying, "look at me, look at me – see where I'm falling short?" Of course not. Save yourself the headache later; mandate their participation now. Without full participation of all units, every report that displays rankings and comparisons (e.g., store, region, company, team, etc.) will be incomplete. **Make customer feedback and measurement a "brand standard" of your company.**

> *If you make customer feedback measurement optional, you are sending a message that customer service is also optional!*

4. **TAKE ACTION!** As the old saying goes, "When all is said and done, more is usually said than done!"* Here is the bottom line:

> *Use* the information.
> *Fix* the problems.
> *Celebrate* the positives.
> *Improve* the employees and the processes.

Then *repeat the cycle*. Since the only meaningful measures of long-term satisfaction are repeat purchase and referrals, then all efforts should be focused on delighting each customer so he/she will return again and tell their friends. This brings us back, once again, to a basic principle:

"Spectacular achievement is always preceded by unspectacular preparation."**

Superior customer service is hard, repetitive, and sometimes tedious work, but it's exactly that effort that makes the difference!

PRACTICAL TACTICS: (Questions to ponder)

Are "hard" statistical measurements an integral part of your company? Are you still relying only on external, third-party mystery shopping, or have you begun using surveys to collect **actual customer experience feedback**? Is customer satisfaction measurement a "nice-to-have," or have you mandated it across your organization? Is feedback consistently delivered to each level of the organization? Are you doing anything with the feedback after you collect it? Do you require follow-up action?

---

* *(Attributed to Lou Holtz)*
** *(Attributed to Robert H. Schuller)*

"What to measure?"

Components of quality: knowing where to aim!

OK, it's time to start measuring. What should you measure? I have a simple rule I use to answer this question. Remember the Platinum Rule of Service that we discussed earlier? That's what I measure. I measure the answers to these two questions:

1. What do customers want (product, process, people)?
2. How am I doing in giving them what they want (execution)?

Remember the old adage about understanding a man by first walking a mile in his shoes? This also describes the basics of customer experience measurement. Start with actually "living his experience" and then "measuring that experience."

By the way, when you've walked a mile in another man's shoes, then … (1) you've got his shoes, and (2) you're a mile away so he can't get you. (I love that joke.)

What do customers generally value in a service experience? What do **you** value? Hundreds of research studies have tried to answer that question. Here is a list that I like. (There are many others.) This one comes from a framework developed in the mid-80's called SERVQUAL. Guess what? It too is common sense, but with a well-thought-out framework behind it.

Measuring consumer perceptions of service quality*

1. **Reliability:**   Deliver as promised! Perform the service.
2. **Responsiveness:** Let me know you care – speed, concern, hustle.
3. **Assurance:**   Communication, credibility, security, competence.
4. **Empathy:**   Understanding/knowing the customer, caring.
5. **Tangibles:**   Atmosphere, appearance, etc.

* *(From "Delivering Quality Service; Balancing Customer Perceptions and Expectations," by Zeithaml, Parasuraman & Berry, Free Press, 1990.)*

Here are some example survey questions that clients have used from each of the five areas:

1. **Reliability:** "How was the taste/haircut/car rental/class/photo, etc.?"
2. **Responsiveness:** "Did we deliver the ____ in the time frame you expected?"
3. **Assurance:** "Did we take ownership of your issue? Do you trust us? Were we polite?"
4. **Empathy:** "Did we listen and show concern for your situation?"
5. **Tangibles:** "Was the store clean and inviting?"

These are the basic items that determine a customer's eventual satisfaction with your company. But customers' needs and wants change continually – you need to measure their experiences in real time, and you must be flexible and try to anticipate their needs.

By engaging the customer in providing feedback about each of these areas, you will be getting a more complete picture of your performance.

PRACTICAL TACTICS: (Questions to ponder)

Do you know what your customers want? Are you measuring customer perceptions in at least the five basic areas presented above?

Surveys: methods and timing

Make customer feedback convenient, anonymous, unbiased, immediate, and actionable

What survey methods work best? Should we conduct mall intercepts as customers leave a store? Should we provide comment cards on each table in a restaurant? Should we call them at home, during the dinner hour?

Face-to-face or ear-to-ear survey methods surely would provide the most accurate, least biased, most immediate response possible, right? In theory, yes. In practice, no.

Humor me for a minute, and take a little quiz with me. At a restaurant, one member of your party orders the spinach salad, and gets some spinach stuck in her teeth. On a scale of 1 to 10 rate the probability that you will *tell* that person *to her face* about the "meal" (stuck between her teeth) that she is "saving for later?"

Would you tell them about the stuck spinach?

If the person is...	No Way!			Possibly				Absolutely!		
...a potential client	1	2	3	4	5	6	7	8	9	10
...an actual client	1	2	3	4	5	6	7	8	9	10
...a co-worker	1	2	3	4	5	6	7	8	9	10
...a friend	1	2	3	4	5	6	7	8	9	10
...a family member	1	2	3	4	5	6	7	8	9	10
...your spouse	1	2	3	4	5	6	7	8	9	10

☐ - Typical answer set

So, what does this little exercise tell us?

Generally, all other things being equal, most people are "chicken." They are *conflict avoiders!* Most folks would rather stick a fork in their head than tell you bad news to your face, particularly if they don't know you.

Let's turn our attention now to the *timing* of the feedback. Historically, companies have been willing to settle for customer feedback, delivered to company senior management, all packaged up in a nice thick report, statistics neatly outlined, and presented with great fanfare two to three months after the fact. Those days are gone! In a world where teenagers are sending text messages before service experiences are even completed, receiving customer feedback on anything but a real-time basis is unacceptable.

I often use an analogy comparing the weekend *"College Football Top-25 Poll"* to the *headset* that the coaches wear on the sideline during the game. Both tools give the coach needed feedback. But one gives him immediate, actionable, person-specific feedback. Some customer feedback vendors believe that the goal of customer experience management is to simply create high-level ranked lists of unit performance at the end of each week, like the Top-25 rankings. I believe that a customer feedback tool should provide *real-time, actionable information – at a detailed level – "during the game!"*

So, where can we find a feedback method that is accurate, real-time, anonymous, minimizes bias, and is cost effective? I believe the best current feedback choices are: *automated phone, web, and mobile-device surveys.* Some vendors offer good old traditional agent-guided phone interviews as a preferred method over automated surveys of any kind. I disagree. While there are some occasions where personal phone interviews are ideal, usually the much higher cost outweighs any benefits. Also, the presence of an interviewer causes respondents to lean toward socially acceptable answers. (Remember the previous spinach example?) This is called social desirability bias, or sometimes conflict avoidance. So, while less personal, an automated survey is usually more immediate, almost always less biased, and more cost effective – leading to more surveys per budgeted dollar spent.

The next question we might ask is this: *Can I use automated phone, web, and/or mobile-device surveys together?* The answer to this question is a little more complex. The use of mixed methods sequentially has generally been accepted as a way to increase response rates without increasing bias or error. (For example, using an automated out-bound dialer to contact a respondent and then directing them to a web site to take the survey.) However, using mixed methods at the same time (e.g., allowing a customer to choose between a toll-free phone number and a web survey), has been debated by academics for several reasons. Firstly, people tend to perceive questions differently when they *see* them versus when they *hear* them.

(Respondents are more likely to spread their answers out over a 5 point scale when they see the questions. If they are asked the questions on the phone, they may tend to gravitate toward the end-points of the question.) Secondly, in the early Internet days, web usage was skewed, as the elderly, and less affluent households were not well represented.

Notwithstanding the above arguments, I firmly believe that *the benefits of using mixed methods of collecting surveys outweigh the potential negatives.* Here is my reasoning:

1. The more methods used, the more convenient for the customer, and the more surveys collected. *(This is called a reduction in non-response bias.)*

2. Using a mixture of survey collection methods reduces sampling error by collecting more surveys. *(Since precision is a function of sample size, the larger the sample, the smaller the error.)*

3. Having multiple survey choices increases the probability of immediacy to the experience.

4. Online skewing is not as problematic as it once was, as Internet usage has become widespread.

5. For the large majority of survey uses, the fact that different survey methods may slightly favor different answers is usually not a problem anyway, as long as the approximate mix between methods is maintained, thereby keeping the data comparable over time.

The debate over this small point reminds me of high school debate class – tell me which side you want me to take, and I will argue its merits. The truth is, that as we measure customer experiences, we need to guard ourselves against going overboard with too much emphasis on statistical biases, sampling errors, and the like, because our goal is to give the customer the most convenient methods for them to provide us immediate *operational feedback* that we can then *take action on* to improve our service. If you have a market research and statistical background, you may find the first part of the previous sentence slightly heretical. Believe me, I understand issues of bias, sampling, and statistical significance. But we need to keep reminding ourselves of the goal of monitoring and measuring the customer experience. (If our goal is to test a one-off hypothesis, extrapolating from a sample to the entire population, then more robust, statistically accurate surveying procedures are required.)

But this is **not** the purpose of customer experience measurement. Its purpose is to allow customers to tell us, through quantitative and qualitative feedback, how we are performing **operationally**, including things we do well and areas where we can improve – both as a company, and at each individual unit. We are looking for immediate, detailed, actionable information.

Occasionally, one of my colleagues or clients will get carried away with some esoteric, academic point of research. That's when we each need to remind ourselves of the following: "No customer cares about the statistics and academics of the survey or its sample size when they interact with a rude clerk, or visit a filthy bathroom, or receive a burned meal." The statistically significant sample size of that population is **one!**

The more dissatisfied customers become, the more likely they will be to tell their friends. Bad experiences seem to be more quickly and more widely shared among customers than good experiences. When companies make it easy for customers to complain, and then handle those complaints, the dissatisfaction felt by the customer starts to fade. So, it is important that customers feel that their issues are heard and that they have had their feelings acknowledged. Additionally, I believe that most customers like to brag to others about people or companies who go out of their way to provide consistently superior service. Your goal should be to choose a collection method that is easy for customers to use, minimizes bias, provides for immediate feedback, and collects data from very happy and not-so-happy customers (and everyone in between). At the time of this writing, automated phone, web, and mobile-device surveys - offered simultaneously - best fit that bill. (In the not too distant future, perhaps more novel survey collection methods may eventually supplement or even displace these.)

PRACTICAL TACTICS: (Questions to ponder)

Are your survey collection methods anonymous, unbiased, and collected in real-time? Are you providing multiple methods for your customers to present their opinions? Have you made it convenient for them to give you their feedback, or do they have to search for a listening ear or feedback line to use?

Surveys: invitations, design, and volume

Designing and presenting effective surveys

Disclaimer 1: I'm going to skim the surface of a very large iceberg in this chapter. In my bookcase, I have over 25 academic books and hundreds of articles dealing with the intricacies of survey design and usage. But I'm just going to present a brief summary here. Why? (1) Trying to cover all that minutiae would take a book 30 times the size of this one, and (2) it makes me tired. I've extracted some of the important points, so you won't have to.

Disclaimer 2: No survey is foolproof. No market research technique is foolproof. Every methodology has flaws and bias. (Any advisor you work with should be willing to acknowledge that up front.) I strongly advise you to temper your survey results with common sense and your own experience. Survey data should be used ***as a tool*** to aid you in decision making, not make decisions for you.

Survey Methodology

In the previous chapter, I presented my reasons for preferring automated phone, web, and mobile-device surveys over other collection methods. I also presented a case for using several collection methods together to increase response rates. The table below outlines some of the strengths and weaknesses of the phone and web collection methods. (Mobile device pros and cons closely parallel the web, with the obvious added benefit of mobility.)

Phone (IVR) Surveys	Web Surveys
Nearly everyone has a phone, and initiating a survey is very simple.	Not every customer has web access or is willing to take the time to log in, etc.
Multi-select questions are more difficult ("choose all that apply…").	Multi-select questions are more easily incorporated.
Voice messages capture customer emotions and are easily integrated.	Text messages are easily captured.
Customers cannot pause a survey.	Customers can pause in the middle of a survey.
More immediate, feedback received soon after service experience.	Typically, more time elapses between the service experience and survey.
Shorter. Focused.	More detail can be collected, including research, marketing, and demographics.

Survey Invitation and Solicitation

General

Depending on what kind of customer experience you will be measuring, you may choose to *passively* invite customers to respond, or you may decide to *actively* solicit participation. In either case, you will want to have the survey invitation presented to the customer in as many ways as possible in order to maximize exposure. Regardless of the primary method of invitation, using a second method will generally increase response rates. You should keep instructions as simple as possible, using a bulleted outline and emphasizing that the survey is quick and easy to take.

Avoid "home cookin' "

The best invitation methods are those that cannot be directly affected by the employee in any way. (If the person presenting the survey invitation is allowed to choose who gets an invitation, customers that had a bad experience may not be offered the survey.) Sometimes it isn't possible to completely automate the invitation (for example, technical issues with point-of-sale systems in a retail store, or old switching technology in a call center can hinder automation). However, every effort should be made to avoid "selective handouts," whereby employees could withhold surveys from disgruntled customers.

Passive invitation to take a survey

In retail or home services settings, I recommend printing the survey invitation on the front or back of the receipt or invoice whenever possible. As each customer finishes their survey, they are given an incentive code to write down, thereby "activating" their receipt and turning it into a valuable coupon. This method automates the process, removes the problems of coupon printing, distribution, and storage, and protects against home cookin'. Some businesses choose to use other methods in addition to the receipt. For example, a company may choose to place labels on a soda cup, issue vouchers, print the invitation on the side of a bag, hang a poster or table banner advertising the survey, print the invitation on an invoice folder, etc. Coupons are often used to capture responses from non-purchasing customers (who didn't receive a receipt).

Actively soliciting feedback

In some instances, for purposes of sampling, or to ensure higher response rates, you may want to actively solicit respondents. The most common method of solicitation is to e-mail people an invitation. Another popular method involves using attended or automated telephone solicitation followed by a transfer to the survey. Other methods include: web banners, mail, fax, etc. If you are going to actively solicit participation in the survey, you will want to: personalize the invitation, clearly identify who you are and how you acquired the respondent's contact information, and allow the customer to opt out of any mailing list or future contact.

"Wait! Wait! Before you storm out, would you please fill out our customer service survey?"

Call center invitation methods

In a call center, best practice methods include: (1) gaining permission, and then calling the customer back with an automated outbound survey soon after the original call, (2) using your IVR to invite the caller to stay on the line, and then automatically transferring the caller to the survey, (3) having the agent offer a pre-scripted invitation, followed by a manual transfer, or (4) if you are capturing emails, an outbound email invitation can automatically be sent following interaction with a call center representative. (Depending upon the sophistication of your call center's infrastructure, method #3 might be the one you initially use until you upgrade your technology.)

Survey Incentives

Do I need to use a survey incentive?

I am often asked if it is necessary to give an incentive to customers who take a survey. The short answer is that it depends on how naturally motivated the customer is to take the survey. Some industries require no incentive at all. (For example, some hospital surveys have response rates of over 65% without any incentive.) As a general rule, the greater the intensity of the service interaction, the less necessary a survey incentive becomes.

The use of incentives helps do several things, it:

1. **Increases response rates,** and

2. **Reduces "non-response bias."**
   (Surveys without an incentive tend to narrowly capture either the 'gripers' or the 'very happy' customers. Using an incentive increases participation from customers in-between the polarized ends, giving you better results.)

I recommend using incentives to capture the broadest possible cross-section of customers.

What incentive should be offered?
Offer incentives that:

- Have value and are worth something in the customers' eyes.
- Have broad appeal across your customer base.
- Stimulate repeat business (bounce backs).
- Stimulate trial of strategic products or categories.

Incentives need not be expensive to generate significant response. Here are a few tips on incentives: "Softer costs," like a free appetizer from a restaurant, a free oil change from a car dealership, or half off a round of golf from a golf course, work well and are the most economical. Dollar-denominated incentives work better than "% off" coupons – (even if they equate to the same amount). Consider non-traditional currencies, such as frequency awards, or airline miles. Sweepstakes incentives sometimes work – but they may skew responses toward a specific demographic.

Success of incentives in driving survey responses

Less Successful Offers	⟵⟶		More Successful Offers	
Sweepstakes	% off next purchase	$'s off next $XX purchase	Free "soft cost" item	$'s off next purchase

Is it important how the invitation is presented?
The invitation and offer must ***STAND OUT*** and attract attention. For example, to make the offer stand out on the point-of-sale receipt:

- Leave *white space* around the offer line.
- *Highlight the offer* (e.g., colored text, **Larger Font**, ALL CAPS).
- Train employees to *circle the offer* and *point it out.*

Remember – simplicity and structure:

- *Use numbers or bullets* in a step-by-step outline format.
- Keep the instructions *as simple as possible.*
- Emphasize the survey is *quick and easy* ("Take a 3-min survey").
- *Avoid lengthy disclaimers* or explanations, if possible.

Sample Receipt
Invitation and Incentive

```
Total payment due:          $15.68


*******************************

FREE DESSERT OR APPETIZER!
      On your next visit


1) Call 1-800-785-7262

          or visit

    www.msharesurvey.com

2) Enter access code: ####

3) Take a brief automated survey

4) Write redemption code:_____
```

* The access code is specific to your company and location.

In some cases, companies have been unable to make modifications to the way POS receipts are printed. In this situation, I recommend some alternatives: (1) pre-print the invitation on the back of the receipt or other items (cups, napkins, bags, etc.), (2) use coupons to supplement the POS receipt, or (3) place posters, tent cards, and other signage.

Incentive redemption and validation

Incentive redemption should be viewed through two different lenses: (1) what is technically possible, and (2) what is actually done in practice. The technical abilities of a vendor like Mindshare can provide for strict enforcement of incentive fulfillment. For example, customer redemption codes can be verified against detailed information produced by the system.

But, the large majority of companies do not actually validate redemption codes when the customer turns in the coupon or receipt. Why not?

- Operationally, it can be challenging to "check each number" while a line of customers is waiting.
- Do you really want to publicly reject a customer trying to redeem?
- System fraud controls, if used properly, will thwart or discourage all but the most egregious theft.
- Most companies use incentives that actually bring in incremental business or at the least serve as "bounce back" coupons. They want all the business they can get. (For example, generating 2–3 incremental entrees is easily worth giving away a free appetizer.)

The cost of incentive redemption

One of my pet peeves in measuring customer feedback is the whining that sometimes accompanies the redemption of incentives. Occasionally I'll hear a unit operator say something like, "The cost of the incentives is killing me!" *But is it, really?*

Let's review some of the reasons for implementing a customer feedback system:

1. Continuous improvement of unit operations.
2. Developing loyal customers leading to increased revenues.
3. Remote monitoring 24/7 – your customers become full-time "mystery shoppers."
4. The survey invitation itself becomes a bounce-back coupon, bringing customers back.

Whenever companies do a cost/benefit analysis of measuring the customer experience, it is overwhelmingly clear that the benefits significantly outweigh the minimal costs, including incentive redemption costs. Some clients have been so conservative in their analysis that they required the customer feedback system to make money as a bounce back coupon alone, excluding benefits 1, 2, and 3 above, which are the biggest long-term generators of incremental revenue. This **significantly understated** the value of measuring the customer experience – but the analysis showed that the company still made a *3-times multiple* on its net investment, even with "both hands tied behind its back!" Would you spend $20.00 to make $60.00 in incremental revenues? Of course you would!

To complete the full analysis, one would subtract the incremental cost of the survey system, subtract variable product costs, and add in estimated incremental revenues created by:

- A consistently-improving service offering.
- Loyal, repeat customers, served by loyal, productive employees.
- The ability to monitor customer feedback daily.

The end result is an absolutely convincing return on investment!
Annual returns of clients have ranged from 3X to 16X+ multiples on total investment, including redemptions! And, those are only the short-term results. (Also see the chapter titled: "Measuring the ROI," page 168)

Survey Design *(a few summarized tips)*

The details of survey design are outside the scope of this book. However, I have listed here a few general "rules of thumb" to jumpstart your thinking.

- Keep the survey short to avoid survey fatigue. Every department will want to add "pet" questions. Avoid the temptation to create an "all things for all people" survey. You can't "boil the ocean;" you must learn to say "No," and focus your questions. Target phone survey length at a maximum of approximately 3–4 minutes, and web surveys at 4–7 minutes.
- Concentrate on the major areas you can control: people, product, environment, and process.
- Keep questions short and pointed.
- Limit each question to address only one variable. (For example, "Was your server friendly and helpful?" incorrectly asks two questions.)
- Only ask a question if the answer can drive action.
- Avoid asking questions that "lead the witness."
- Ask a few open-ended questions to supplement quantitative results, and hear the actual "voice of the customer." Open-ended responses provide the highest granularity and the most actionable information at the unit level. Choose a system that lets you easily listen to the customer's voice.
- For phone surveys: repeat the scale meanings frequently. Keep surveys shorter for post-call center surveys.
- For web surveys: ask more specific questions, but don't overwhelm. Size the text boxes to suggest a limit on length of open-ended question responses. Use section headings.
- Be sure and say "Thank you" at the end.
- **Advanced survey design topics (beyond this book) include:** question types, question ordering, bias, scale design, endpoint anchoring, dispersion, segmentation, conditional branching, cross tabs, filtering, and many other topics. (This is why you should call in the experts.)

Survey Volume

It is impossible to discuss survey volume without mentioning statistics. This means that almost no one will be happy. Experts may find the following discussion too shallow, and the rest will skip this chapter altogether. So, to make it more palatable, I'll just focus on a few practical statistics dealing with survey volume.

How many responses should we target?

> **Rule #1:** There is no magic formula for determining the right number of responses to collect.
>
> **Rule #2:** It's a little bit science and a little bit art.

There are two main considerations when determining how many responses to collect.

1. **Statistical estimation of the population from a sample:**
   Sampling *a few* of your customers to try and estimate what *all* of your customers are feeling – this is useful for discrete surveys and "relationship" surveys, like market research, demographics, new product introduction, etc.
   (Short answer: Try for at least 100 responses per unit, per survey cycle to achieve roughly a 10% margin of error.)

2. **Representative sampling of operations:**
   How many responses are needed to gauge how well *each of your stores/employees is performing* each day – often called a "transactional" or "event" survey?
   (Short answer: Try for about 100 responses per unit/month – depending on customer count.)

Let me provide some additional explanation about each area:

1. Statistical estimation of the population from a sample ("Market research-type" surveys)

Any estimate from a survey sample is unlikely to exactly equal the true population's feelings for a variety of reasons (e.g., "luck of the draw." Is the sample random or diverse enough, etc.?)

Because of this, two <u>conflicting expectations</u> will need to be balanced:

➕ 1. The *larger the sample* size the greater the probability that the sample will represent the population.

➖ 2. At some point, the additional benefit of more surveys is *not worth the extra cost.*

The major statistical issue for this type of surveying is, "How much precision is needed to make appropriate decisions?"

Two primary variables describe the level of precision available. They are: *margin of error* and *confidence level.*

You've probably heard a statement like:

"65% of voters favor Daniel Duff for Mayor"

(+/- 5% at a 95% confidence level)

The (+/- 5%) in the statement is the "margin of error," and the 95% is the level of confidence. In the above example, it means the pollsters have 95% confidence that somewhere between 60% and 70% of the whole population favors Daniel Duff for Mayor. Most statisticians use a 95% confidence interval.

What about the margin of error? The most crucial factor affecting the margin of error is the sample size. *Regardless of population size, a sample size of 100 will produce a margin of error of approximately 10%.* Beyond a sample of 100 responses, there are diminishing returns to reducing the margin of error by increasing the sample size. For example, at 500, the margin of error is 4.5%, at 1,000 the margin of error is about 3%.

A margin of error of 10% at a 95% confidence level suggests a sample survey size of approximately 100 surveys per operating unit.

Approximately 100 surveys is my recommendation for your target if you are using discrete or "relationship" surveys using statistical sampling.

2. Representative sampling of operations ("Operations monitoring or transactional" surveys)

This is the type used for most customer feedback surveys, and the type I reference throughout this book. Its primary goal is to allow the customer to help improve your operations by becoming more engaged with you. Operational monitoring presents a completely different situation regarding how many responses to collect. One of the major decisions confronting companies in this area is: **"How many customer responses will it take to know if my employees are *delivering service* in the correct way?"**

For example: let's assume you are running a restaurant and you want to know how often your servers are offering an appetizer to each guest. If you have 12 employees, you'll want to have at least 7–10 measurements per employee, each month, or a range of 84–120 completed surveys per month.

Another example: you run a salon and can't get your stylists to recommend the retail hair-care products to customers. An operational monitoring survey will ask each surveyed customer, "Did your stylist offer you hair-care products?" Now you'll know stylist compliance with this policy, and the stylists will upsell hair-care products more consistently.

You need to **continuously measure** service **at the local level** to recognize service and product variation – over time, between units, and across individual customers. When companies only "spot check" using statistical samples, they will invariably miss a wide range of performance across their locations, *hidden behind averages*. Variation in the delivery of the service represents a significant risk to companies concerned only with high-level statistical averages, because at the unit level, customers are experiencing inconsistent execution, not high-level averages.*

Aiming for 7–10 measurements per employee per month gives you a representative sample of about one completed survey every third or fourth day, per employee. This is my recommendation for customer experience monitoring surveys.

The Summary ("How many responses?"):
It is both a science and an art to determine the appropriate number of responses to collect from a survey. An important distinction to consider is the difference between collecting enough surveys to estimate the average "feeling" of your customers, and collecting enough surveys to determine how well your local units and your individual employees are executing your policies and standards.

I suggest you aim at collecting about **100 responses per month, per "average" unit.** (This will provide customer feedback with approximately a 10% margin of error.) To measure how well each of your employees is executing your service standards, you may want to collect **more** or **less surveys** – depending upon your desired confidence level and the number of employees and customer counts at each location.

---

* (For more information on local service variation, see "Manage Your Human Sigma" by Fleming, Coffman, Harter, Harvard Business Review, July 2005.)

What is a good response rate?

Response rates vary by industry, channel, awareness of the invitation, proximity to the event, and richness of the incentive. The table that follows shows normalized response rate ranges for one example. (A base of 100 invitations is shown, for ease of comparison.) When passive survey invitations are used, survey response rates usually range from 1% unaided to over 30% using rich incentives and heavy promotion. If active solicitation is used, survey response rates may jump to over 65%.

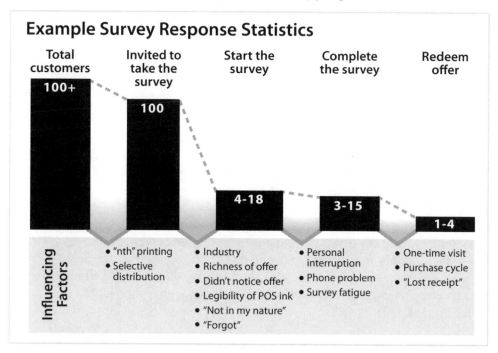

Example Survey Response Statistics

Total customers	Invited to take the survey	Start the survey	Complete the survey	Redeem offer
100+	100	4-18	3-15	1-4

Influencing Factors

- • "nth" printing
- • Selective distribution

- • Industry
- • Richness of offer
- • Didn't notice offer
- • Legibility of POS ink
- • "Not in my nature"
- • "Forgot"

- • Personal interruption
- • Phone problem
- • Survey fatigue

- • One-time visit
- • Purchase cycle
- • "Lost receipt"

Adjusting survey and redemption volumes up or down

Volumes can be controlled through several means:

- • Check the invitation basics: correct information – codes, web address, 800#, etc? Printing dark enough? Clear, highly-visible message?
- • Adjust the "richness" of the incentive offer (a free entrée will drive more surveys than a free soda).
- • Increase or decrease the prominence of the invitation.
- • Use "nth" printing (for example, invite every other customer).
- • Strength of "buy-in" and/or compensation of employees.
- • A forced cap on completed surveys can also be accomplished through either a stub survey (one short question) or a "hard cap" ("Thank you for calling, we have completed the survey collection at this time").

Controlling Fraud and Duplication

Sophisticated survey vendors will have multiple methods available to control fraudulent or duplicate surveys. Some are systemic and some are reinforced by client training – however, **each requires overt communication to the employee** so that they are aware that the controls are in place. Examples of suspicious surveys requiring further investigation might include: multiple surveys from the same phone number or internet address, calls from a store or employee phone, repeat surveys from non-repeat guests, multiple call attempts from one survey invitation, unusual volume spikes, etc.

Methods used to control intentional or accidental abuse include: identifying and filtering invalid surveys through caller ID number and/or internet address comparison, access code algorithms, using unique identifiers, high-score-same-phone number correlations, and unusual score anomalies. Many companies block repeat callers from taking surveys after a pre-determined number of surveys per week or month. In addition, post-survey and post-redemption audits and "data hygiene" processes may be performed on a regular basis to evaluate the source and validity of surveys.

Notwithstanding the sophisticated tools mentioned above, the single most important method of preventing fraud is to let employees and customers know that fraud is being monitored, and that *the consequences of fraudulent behavior by employees will be dismissal*. Knowing that caller ID numbers and redemption codes will be audited is usually enough to stop all but the most flagrant violations.

The execution of fraud controls must be balanced against the desire to be "approachable" and "inviting" to your customers. Said another way, in the area of fraud control, it is important that you *not manage to the exceptions*. Policies should not be put in place to "catch the very last thief," but rather to block the most blatant violations.

Implementing the practices outlined above will prevent the vast majority of intentional and unintentional survey abuses.

PRACTICAL TACTICS: (Questions to ponder)

Did you read this chapter completely? Did you understand it? (Did you answer that last question truthfully?) Have you set expectations that fraud will not be tolerated? Do you see why it's best to leave this stuff to professionals?

Social media

Structuring the unstructured

Social media makes us all publishers and recipients of feedback

Past models of communication

Prior to the invention of the printing press, communication was personal – primarily one-to-one, as people shared their thoughts with family and neighbors. With the advent of commercial printing, down through the age of television, communication morphed into a one-to-many model, and those in charge of publishing were assumed to be reputable, professional, and fair in controlling the content.

Huge changes underway

Social media (SM) is changing everything. Suddenly, not only does virtually everyone on the planet have the ability to reach everyone else, but each of us can now become a "publisher." We can create our own content and distribute it very inexpensively, and no one is controlling the content or checking its accuracy. In summary, communication has dramatically evolved: from one-to-one, to one-to-many, to many-to-many! And, it's still evolving. The changes yet to happen will most assuredly continue to be remarkable. Regarding the future of social media, the only thing I am confident of is that "I don't even know what I don't know!"

Having said that, there are some things I do know, and some current social media best practices. (While SM also has huge potential as a marketing tool, I will focus primarily on customer feedback through social media and company "buzz" on the social media channel.)

Brief background

Although social media can take many different forms, the five examples I'll address below provide a good cross section as it exists today.

> **Blog:** A website where the "blogger" (the blog owner) provides commentary and content, similar to an online diary, and readers may respond by leaving their own comments. Entries are usually displayed in reverse-chronological order.

> **Micro blogging:** Similar to blogging, but limited to short bursts of information, often relating to quick expressions (e.g. "What are you doing right now?").

Social networks: Online communities where people who share interests or are linked in some other way can connect, interact, and share information.

Media sharing: Online websites where users can upload and share videos, music, photographs, and other amateur content.

Wikis: Online, collaborative websites allowing any user to contribute data and edit any page.

Why social media matters
Some companies wrongly assume that SM is merely used by teenagers and young college students. However, Facebook reports that its fastest growing demographic is age 35 and older.* A Cone Business study in social media revealed that of the 60% of Americans using social media, 93% think that a company should have a social media presence, and 85% felt companies should use social media to interact with consumers.**

It's not all useful information
As social media evolves, more individuals are telling those in their SM networks about their product and service experiences. The majority of opinions and ideas shared on social media sites are much less structured than those of a customer taking a phone or web survey, where feedback can be quantified, sorted, classified, and tied to a specific store, employee, or incident. This makes the information from most SM sites difficult to report and act on. Most of the information "floating around out there" is not intended as helpful feedback to companies, or even specific complaints about service lapses, but rather just ad hoc conversational commentary. Social media can also be used as a bully pulpit for gripers, whiners, and even unscrupulous competitors to vent and spread unsubstantiated and vague claims.

There are many tools available to help search social media for postings mentioning a specific company. However, simply spreading a net to collect this information is akin to dredging a stream for fish – while some fish will be captured, so will a lot of old boots, sticks, rocks, hubcaps, and tires.

Similarly, merely collecting unstructured data from the web will provide very little actionable information that can be used to improve a company's strategy or operations. Employing data mining techniques can help further dissect or "bucket" the "buzz" about your company into different categories.

* www.facebook.com/press/info.php?statistics
** www.coneinc.com/content1182

This can be useful at the strategic level. But still you are left with a dearth of specific actionable information. The way to overcome this weakness is to **add structure** to data flowing in from social media networks.

Some **tactical recommendations** to consider about social media:

(1) Get in the game. Establish an SM presence. Contribute.

Set up company accounts with key social media websites (e.g. Facebook, Twitter). As you become more established in the SM world, people will learn where to turn to give you feedback and it will be easier to respond to issues – both good and bad. Become an authentic member of the community by providing helpful tips, announcing promotions, and giving valuable information about new products. The benefit of this approach is that your brand will become a trusted resource in the social media community and your customers will be more likely to come to your SM pages to leave feedback.

(2) Relationships and relevance – not advertising.

Although organizations may be tempted to use SM sites to promote their products or services, SM communities will not accept them if they use the social media sites to advertise using old-fashioned methods. No one wants to follow a company that posts about how wonderful it is followed by links to canned marketing pitches. Social media is all about relationships and relevance. Companies need to participate by adding valuable, relevant information to forums and communities. Furthermore, a person in an organization that has the power to help resolve concerns should respond to a dissatisfied customer in a genuine manner. Unfortunately, there is not a simple, automated way to participate in these communities. There needs to be personal human involvement. While there are various free and paid services that can help a company aggregate the feedback, this does not eliminate the need for an actual person(s) to respond to customers and deal with their concerns. These employees need to have good judgment and strong communication skills, and be empowered to make decisions.

(3) "Structure the unstructured." Gather. Respond. Add Structure.

Casting a net to measure the social "buzz" about your company sounds important and inviting. But simply collecting unstructured comments from social media sites will leave you with a bunch of public postings, but very little actionable information (e.g. Where did the issue happen? Which employee(s) performed poorly? When did this happen? What product was affected?).

You need to be able to:

- **Gather** feedback from unstructured SM sources,
- **Respond quickly** and **personally**, and then
- Give the author an easy way to provide you with **additional, structured information.**

You should watch for raw posts and comments that mention your company. Catching customer complaints early allows you to respond quickly, further engendering customer loyalty. Many free applications make it easy for you to access live SM information. Some examples: (1) a *current "buzz" chart* showing the current amount of online discussion about your company, (2) a *live feed* showing real-time posts and "tweets" about your company, (3) a *social media search bar*, pre-screening all online social media sites for postings about your company, and (4) a *"blog listener,"* consolidating all blogs mentioning your company.

Even with these gathering tools, you will still need to dedicate at least part of an employee's time to filtering and responding to comments and to managing your social media presence. A complaint is an opportunity to demonstrate your dedication to customer service and willingness to listen and respond to customers' concerns. When someone posts a complaint, it may elicit responses from other customers who feel similarly, allowing you to reach out to an entire group.

As you respond to SM feedback personally, I suggest you provide a way for the author to easily give you additional structured information. This is best accomplished by simply **including a link** in your response that directs the author to what I'll call a **"mini-survey,"** for lack of a better term.

Getting anonymous social media authors to take a mini-survey (1-2 minutes) will provide your company with actionable and reportable feedback, rather than the unstructured feedback typical of today's social media communication. You can use this survey to gain more structured information about the customer's issue, such as the location, who was involved, the type of problem, when the problem occurred, and any additional comments to aid in addressing the issue. The data provided from this mini-survey can be **easily integrated** with your existing feedback surveys and presented to your local managers through an integrated enterprise feedback management (EFM) system.

This strategy transforms unstructured comments into structured feedback and actionable information, and delivers it up and down your organizational structure

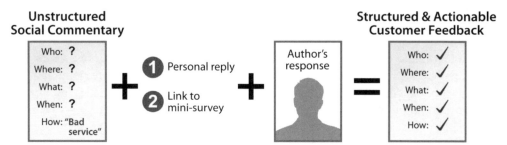

through your existing EFM reporting hierarchy. It also provides your company with a chance to catch negative experiences while the audience is still small.

(4) Make more fans. (Word-of-mouth)

If you are currently gathering customer service feedback, I suggest that you maximize the value of your highly satisfied customers by providing them with SM links at the end of your customer satisfaction survey. These links will give them an easy way to share (on various social media sites) the positive experiences they had with your company. By doing this, you empower people to become advocates of your brand. The easier it is for them to speak out, the more likely they will.

(5) "Fertilize" third-party fan sites about your company.

In addition to establishing your company's own social media presence, you might also consider a strategy of "fertilizing" third-party fan sites about your company, and "seeding" others through marketing incentives.

Beyond improving your marketing efforts, you can also use these third-party fan sites to direct customers toward providing you with structured feedback. The best way to do this is to encourage each third-party site administrator to place a link on their site directing customers to click through and take a mini-survey when they have feedback about your company. By directing fans toward a mini-survey, you can grow the amount of specific, actionable customer feedback you are collecting.

Change
Social media is a rapidly evolving area of customer feedback. Just a few years ago, few had heard of Twitter, and other sites were significantly more popular than Facebook. The reverse is true today. As this book goes to press, Twitter and Facebook are two of the most popular sites. And today's top sites may be replaced by new ideas being created as you read this.

Resource challenges create an impasse
The growth of social media networks creates a very difficult resource allocation challenge for most organizations. With potentially millions of customers "holding a microphone," social media presents a love-hate relationship for businesses that are trying to collect all the customer feedback they can, but are unable to handle the crushing load of social media comments about their company without adding headcount.

Is more structure inevitable?
Like all business problems at an impasse, sooner or later something will have to give. My belief is that eventually, those SM authors who desire follow-up and change will become "trained" to provide companies with feedback in a more automated and structured way. This is not dissimilar to other marketplace "trainings" that have occurred – getting money from a wall rather than a bank teller (ATM), or taking food to your table and cleaning up after yourself (quick-serve restaurants). Similarly, the current "wide open west" of social media **as a feedback tool** is destined to acquire more structure. The recommendations presented in this chapter move in that direction.

PRACTICAL TACTICS: (Questions to ponder)

Are you educating yourself on social media? Have you recognized its power as a feedback tool? Are you listening and responding to this channel? Which of the recommendations above can you start implementing today?

EFM: bringing it all together

Integrating feedback across all touch points

It is vital to continuously gather feedback from any source the customer touches. Your goal should be to make it easy for anyone to provide feedback as their opinions are being formed. The process of systematically gathering feedback and information from multiple stakeholders, analyzing it, and then disseminating it correctly has many different names (e.g. VOC, CEM, CFS, EFM, EF). I'll use the term: enterprise feedback management (EFM).*

The summary graphic on the right outlines the three most important steps of the enterprise feedback management process. Focus should be on (1) collecting feedback (and other information) from as many sources as possible, (2) analyzing it, and then (3) distributing the consolidated and actionable information to the accountable line manager, in real time.

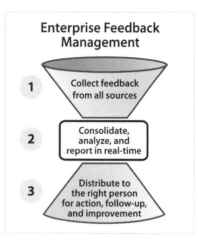

1. Collecting feedback from all sources

In order to ensure that **all** employees are delivering your brand promise, and that customers' expectations are being met or exceeded, you will need to acquire and compile an integrated, holistic view of how customers and others are being treated across all parts of your business. The chart below lists *example* **stakeholders** and **channels** where feedback can be collected.

EFM Potential Applications

Customer	Employee	Social Media
In-store retail	Employee satisfaction	Social networking pulse
Internet homepage	Hiring and tracking	Social feedback & blogs
Website experience	Performance reviews	
Call center (support/sales)	Training	**Vendor/Partner**
Relationship measurement	Course evaluation	Compliance measurement
	Exit interviews	Relationship measurement
Market Research	Ethics and culture	
Product experience		**Compliance & QC Audits**
Enhancement requests	**Data Collection**	Mystery shops
New product evaluation	Registrations	Internal quality audits
Customer demographics	Risk assessment	Process performance

---

* *(Multiple definitions, acronyms, and claims of authorship exist for the individual principles discussed here. In this book I will use "enterprise feedback management" to apply to my definition. See graphic above.)*

2. Consolidating, analyzing, and reporting in real time

After the feedback is collected, it needs to be analyzed for important insights and then presented in a consolidated and easy-to-understand format, where important issues can be easily spotted. Without this step, feedback data is often presented in pieces, providing a disjointed, confusing picture to the local manager. By the time he tries to manually pull the data together, he will have wasted time and probably missed some important insights.

Additional information, such as *financial, demographic,* and *transactional data,* can be automatically appended to the feedback data at this point, thus presenting a more complete picture of the customer's total experience. Tailored reports can then be disseminated to each level of the company.

The graphic below illustrates the consolidation of feedback from five example sources and its integration into a single report.

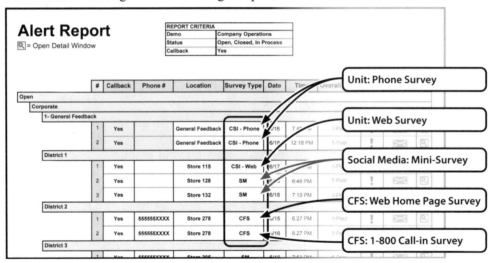

3. Distributing to the right person for action, follow-up, and improvement

The next step ensures that the information is immediately available to front-line managers to *improve operations.* It should be widely accessible up and down the organization's hierarchy, with different reports, roles, and permission levels available for different types of users. With this kind of real-time feedback, managers have a tool to make an immediate impact. When customers and employees see or hear that their feedback is actually being used, they become more invested as an emotional "owner" of the business, which makes them feel more attached and loyal.

An important step in the process is to ensure that someone is **held accountable** for **following up** on each piece of feedback (regardless of how the customer, vendor, or employee chooses to deliver it). Supervisors should also monitor the timing and delivery of corrective actions. Another best practice is to *instantly alert managers* when service breaks down so that recovery can begin immediately.

How EFM fits with existing business processes and systems

EFM is not just a piece of software – it is a way of doing business, and goes hand in hand with a customer-centric culture. It is often used in conjunction with a company's **balanced scorecard** and its customer relationship management **(CRM)** systems. EFM solutions should also be used to help deliver better *internal* service, tying into **help desks** and other **HR** areas. Because the insights represent the feelings and perceptions from the customer's own mind, information gleaned can provide valuable input into a company's CRM system by appending information about *attitudes* to information about *behaviors* and *transactions* already stored in typical CRM systems. If CRM tells you the "what, where, and when," EFM tells you the "how and why."

Benefits of the EFM approach

A well-designed, properly executed EFM solution provides numerous benefits, but it is especially useful in helping a company understand its relationships with customers, employees, suppliers, and others, regarding key issues and concerns, and positive feedback. Some specific examples of the benefits of EFM include:

- Enabling real-time, customer-driven response.
- Understanding the key drivers that keep customers returning.
- Pinpointing specific store/team/employee training needs.
- Ensuring service-lapse recovery – fixing problems so they don't recur.
- "Saving" customers (and their lifetime value) before they permanently defect.
- Compensating employees based directly on customer measurements.
- Providing integrated feedback reporting from each touchpoint.
- Linking satisfaction to loyalty to financial results.

Robust EFM systems provide additional benefits by allowing companies to leverage data across departments or functions. For example, transactional surveys can be augmented with additional market research-oriented questions, thereby saving time and resources. Effective EFM systems also integrate quantitative results (statistically-oriented) with qualitative data (such as verbatim, voice-of-the-customer comments). In this way, the more scientific, quantitative data can be cross-referenced with qualitative data that "speaks" more to the heart.

Here to stay

Enterprise feedback management is not a "fad," a "thing," or a "system." It is a management process that enables organizations to collect feedback in real time through multiple channels and multiple data sources, consolidate feedback from customers, employees, and other stakeholders, integrate that feedback with other important financial and transactional data, use intelligent analytics to turn that data into actionable information, and distribute that information to the right person at the right time for follow up. These concepts are rapidly being adopted as a best practice among leading organizations and are setting companies apart. **It is a part of how they do business every day.**

Tying it all together

The following chart demonstrates what the flow of information can look like after an EFM solution has been implemented. Notice the feedback flowing in from multiple stakeholders, through a variety of channels. The data is consolidated and then transformed into actionable information before being distributed to both executive management and to the accountable manager at the local level.

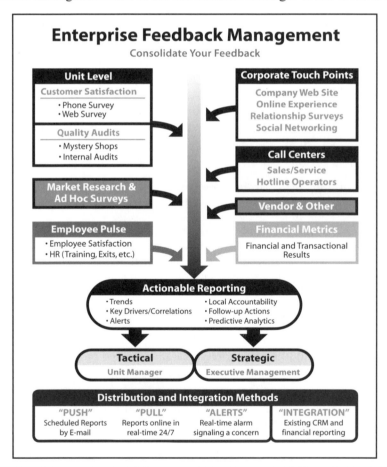

PRACTICAL TACTICS: (Questions to ponder)

Are you enabling customers to respond at all touch points? Is the feedback from various methods brought together in a cohesive, holistic manner, so that local-level managers can see the entire picture of their outlet from the customers' viewpoint?

Continuous quality improvement!

Lather, rinse, and repeat!

(Quality is a <u>movie</u> of continuous improvement, not a <u>snapshot</u>)

I'm told that for years and years the most feared words in the automotive business were:

"Introducing The New Accord!"

Why? Because Honda has been relentless at continuous improvement. They have been the masters at listening to their customers. To companies like Honda, Toyota, Intel, and Apple, success is not a single accomplishment, it's an ongoing process.

Commitment to Improve!

Lather, Rinse, Repeat!

They develop true customer loyalty. Then, when they believe they have succeeded, they tear things down and begin again. Why? Because they know that what worked yesterday will probably not work tomorrow.

Not only do you have to exceed a customer's expectation, but you have to be constantly improving. I call this

"Lather – Rinse – Repeat!"

All the great companies are "learning companies." They listen. They challenge themselves. They improve, and then they repeat the cycle.

On my wall I keep a framed quote attributed to Michelangelo in the last years of his life:

ANCORA IMPARO:
"I am still learning"

This quote inspires me.

I love that attitude. After all, they say "it's what you learn *after you know it all* that really counts."* So, let's say you are pretty darn good. Your customer scores are in the high 90s and you're ravaging the competition. Slack off? Chill? Nope! If you're relentless, then here are some questions for you to ask your customers:

- **What can we do to serve your needs *even better?***
- **How can we *improve our responsiveness*?**

I've had one or two clients tell me that they want to turn customer feedback surveys off after a couple of years, because, "We've heard it all." Once, I even had a CEO of a major U.S. corporation say he didn't really care what customers think, because, "We already know what our customers need."

What a knucklehead! What hubris! Think of the companies that have failed and slithered away because they didn't understand their customers' changing needs. Or, how about this: think of the many successful companies that missed huge opportunities because they didn't listen to their customers closely. Two of the more oft-quoted examples: if Union Pacific had realized that they were in the transportation business, rather than the train business, we might all be flying on Union Pacific Airlines. If Sports Illustrated had thought outside the magazine medium earlier, perhaps we'd be watching "Sports Center" on SITV rather than ESPN.

> *"It's not enough to do this once or twice and then go back to your old ways – you must make this a part of your routine."*
>
> Client

The key to continuous improvement is continuous learning and continuous measurement. I've always believed:

That which gets measured one time improves.
That which gets measured *continuously*, improves *exponentially!*

PRACTICAL TACTICS: (Questions to ponder)

Are you taking a movie of customer service, or simply snapshots? Is yours a learning organization? Are you willing to tear apart even your most successful offerings to make them even better?

---

* (Unknown. Variously attributed to John Wooden and Earl Weaver among others.)

Part IV

Analyzing the Results

Turning data into useful information

"I love math... except for the numbers part"

As a long-time "quant jock" and "numbers guy," here is my take on this important subject. ***If you're not going to use the data you've collected, then "take your ball and go home."*** Don't waste your time or money. I am amazed at the people who understand the theories and capture the customer data, but then don't want to invest the time to learn how to evaluate the results, determine the implications, and act on them.

This subject could fill another book. I'll hit the highlights:

1. Data Types

First, we will examine several basic types of data that you'll be using to evaluate your customers' experiences.

TYPE OF DATA	EXAMPLES OF USE
Absolute metric:	• *82%* of customers were greeted immediately.
Relative: -vs. peers	• We are *4 points below the other store* in our city.
-vs. goals	• It was a good week for us, but we're still *2% points under budget* this quarter.
-vs. benchmarks	• Good news, we are *3% above the region average.*
-vs. competitors	• We have improved our *market share by 6%.*
Relative, over time:	• We have declined 2% points *since last month.*
Causal & non-causal relationships:	• Customers "greeted immediately" are *also* 80% more likely to return. *(Probably causal)*
	• The increase in customer alerts is *correlated* to our increased advertising. *(Probably not causal)*
Combination metrics:	• Various combinations of the above.

The many varying types of analyses that will be performed will determine the exact type of data you will be using.

2. *Kinds of Analyses*

Let's review a few of the various kinds of analyses that can be used to understand the data and draw out specific action steps that will drive operational improvement.

(The arbitrary levels I've assigned (one, two, three) have no intrinsic meaning other than to separate the general skill level (and the time) required to explore and discover the subtle or even faint conclusions hidden in the data.)

<u>Level One</u> *(Fairly straightforward)*

Raw scores, rankings, and lists
(e.g., units and employees, geographies, pieces and parts)
- Simple presentation of the results
- Highest performers vs. peers or vs. goals
- Lowest performers vs. peers or vs. goals
- Comparing performers across attributes

Trending over time
- Directional patterns over time
- Comparison vs. goals or vs. benchmark

Distributions and histograms
- Outlining the distribution of answer responses
- Comparing parts of a whole

Matrix
- Comparing two or more variables for easy quadrant classification (e.g., importance vs. performance)

Unit-oriented
- Reports and analysis created specifically for location or team managers to run their operations

<u>Level Two</u> *(A bit more difficult)*

Basic correlations and regressions
- Determining the strength and direction of relationships between two or more variables
- Identifying potential cause and effect relationships between inputs and desired outcomes

Key drivers
- Discovering the primary drivers of customers' willingness to recommend and/or to return
- Evaluating performance against key drivers (entire company and/or individual unit results)

Benchmarking
- Comparing results either internally across groupings, or externally across competitors, etc.

Cross-tabs and filters
- Matrix presentation of multiple variables: allows for filtering data based on specific combinations of variable inputs
- Most often used to break down information into more granular parts, based on specific variables (e.g. how satisfied were first-time guests?)

Combination presentations
- Using single presentations to show multiple pieces of information

Level Three (Sometimes easy to miss)

Teasing out the "more subtle nuances"

Causal relationships
> (e.g., relationships between employee loyalty, customer loyalty, repurchase, and financial performance)

More complex regressions, distributions, and multivariable combinations
> (e.g., distinguishing "price-of-entry" services vs. "must have" services, penalty-reward-contrast analysis, etc.)

3. Analytical Examples

In this section, for each kind of analysis, I will present a brief synopsis of the type of analysis and data, and then provide several examples of the kinds of graphs and tables that can be used to present the information. (See disclaimers in back of the book, page 200.)

Level One Analysis

Raw Scores, Rankings, and Lists

The most basic and most often used presentation of analytical data
(e.g., units and employees, geographies, pieces, and parts).

- Simple presentation of results
- Highest performers vs. peers or vs. goals
- Lowest performers vs. peers or vs. goals
- Comparing performers across attributes

Ranking, highest performer(s)

Encourage even higher performance.

Highest Ranked Performers

Goal: Learn from and share best practices of these performers.

Units	Service Rating	Product Rating
Oak Street	94 ↑	93 ↑
Maple Street	89 ↑	87
Poplar Street		85
Elm Street	69	71
Ash Street	62	63
Apple Street	52 ↓	61
Cherry Street	48 ↓	59 ↓
Sequoia Street	47 ↓	56 ↓

Ranking, lowest performer(s)

"Whip the horse, team up a weak horse with a strong horse, or get a new cowboy."

Lowest Ranked Performers

Goal: Move these up to at least an average ranking.

Units	Service Rating	Product Rating
Oak Street	94 ↑	93 ↑
Maple Street	89 ↑	87
Poplar Street	81	85
Elm Street	69	71
Ash Street		63
Apple Street	52 ↓	61
Cherry Street	48 ↓	59 ↓
Sequoia Street	47 ↓	56 ↓

Ranking, measured against company standards

Give notice that results are below standard. Search for underlying cause.

Lowest Ranked Performers

Goal: Move these up to company standard. Raise the bar over time.

Units	Service Rating	Product Rating
Oak Street	94 ↑	93 ↑
Maple Street	89 ↑	87
Poplar Street	81	85
Elm Street	69	71
Ash Street	62	63
Apple Street	52 ↓	61
Cherry Street	48 ↓	59 ↓
Sequoia Street	47 ↓	56 ↓

Comparing two front-line employees – across multiple variables

Comparing performance across multiple variables.

Who Are Your Best Performing Employees?

Goal: To pinpoint training needs. In this case, upselling.

	Bob*	Judy*	Difference
Average Score	88	95	7
Greeted Promptly	86	100	14
Friendly Clerk	88	93	5
Attentiveness of Clerk	86	99	13
Offer Accessories	55	83	28
Recommend Matching Items	26	65	39
Clerk Knowledge	88	97	9
Merchandise Variety	91	95	4
Definitely Return	92	100	8
Definitely Recommend	83	99	16
# of Surveys	12	13	

Two clerks, same clothing store, same approx. number of surveys, same time period.

Trending Over Time

Trend charts are used to look for **directional patterns** over time. They are also often used to compare specific stores or groupings of stores to company averages and to track results versus goals.

Trend graph, example 1

Presenting recent trend, store ranking, and improvement.

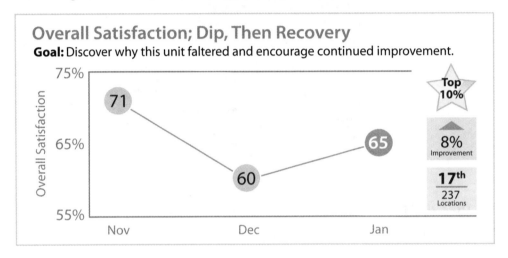

Trend graph, example 2

Comparing store trend vs. internal and external benchmarks.

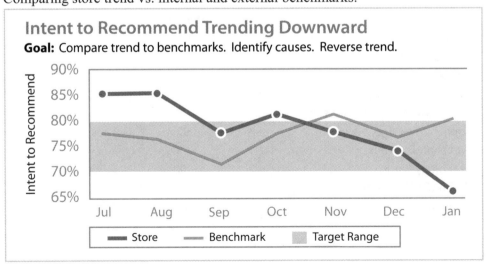

Distributions and Histograms

Comparing distribution of answer responses, and/or comparing parts of a whole.

Histogram

Presenting the distribution of survey responses by question.

Response Distribution

Goal: Review the distributions of answers from all respondents.

Question	Response		% of Responses	# of Responses
Which day did we serve you?	Today	▇	20%	62/308
	Yesterday	▇	16%	49/308
	Another Day	▇▇▇	64%	197/308
Rate the look and feel of the restaurant.	Excellent	▇▇▇	61%	188/308
	Above Avg.	▇▇	26%	80/308
	Average	▍	8%	25/308
	Below Avg.	▏	3%	9/308
	Poor	▏	2%	6/308
Rate the overall value of your dining experience.	Excellent	▇▇▇	75%	231/308
	Above Avg.	▇	20%	62/308
	Average	▍	4%	12/308
	Below Avg.		0%	0/308
	Poor	▏	1%	3/308

Pie chart

Presenting those attributes that are triggering service alerts.

Service Alerts

Goal: Identify the attributes triggering service alerts.

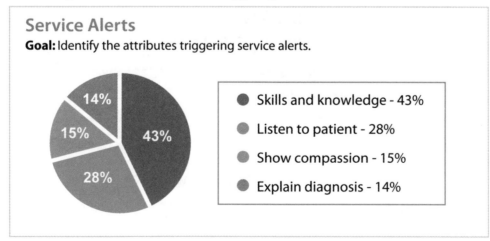

● Skills and knowledge - 43%

● Listen to patient - 28%

● Show compassion - 15%

● Explain diagnosis - 14%

Distributions and Histograms *(continued)*

Bar chart, example 1

Showing a drop in performance during the busiest time of the day.

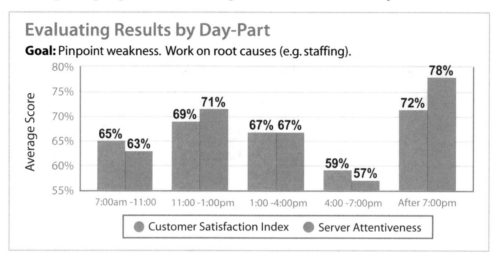

Bar chart, example 2

Demonstrating change in customer satisfaction at various store music levels.

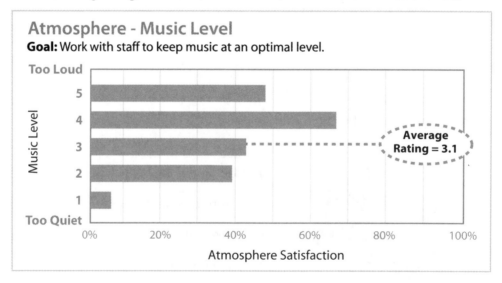

Matrix

Comparing two or more variables for easy quadrant classification.
(e.g., importance vs. performance, or raw score vs. change in score)

Matrix chart, example 1

Graphing performance of retail stores on "wait time" vs. "change in wait time."

Matrix chart, example 2

Importance vs. performance across various attributes.

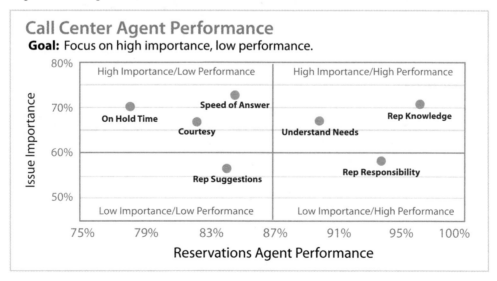

Unit-Oriented

Reports created specifically for unit managers to run their operations.

*Almost all analytical tools can be used individually at the local unit level. However, **combination reports** (such as the one shown below) can be created especially for unit management to focus in on hot issues without wasting time wading through reports.*

Unit scorecard

Presenting survey scores, with comparison to peers, region, company, and top performers, trends, and cross-tabs of important variables (e.g., time of day).

CSI Report*

Key: ▨ Poor   ▣ Acceptable   ▨ Excellent

CSI Index	74.6	Current Month	Previous Month	District 7	All Stores	Top 10% CSI Index
		74.6	61.2	76.1	73.1	96.9
Overall Sat		67.1	66.1	70.4	66.7	96.3
Return		77.8	66.3	80.9	79.5	97.5
Recommend		79.0	51.3	77.0	73.2	96.8
Customer Service Score		**68.5**	**67.8**	**73.0**	**70.6**	**85.5**
Greeting		67.2	59.5	71.7	64.7	94.6
Friendliness		75.0	69.6	78.3	78.6	85.0
Speed of Service		69.2	73.4	70.1	63.5	95.1

Time of day?	Overall	Taste	Appearance	Accuracy	Speed	Recommend
Before 2 p.m.	67.9	66.7	80.8	85.0	42.1	82.1
2 p.m. - 5 p.m.	66.7	68.4	57.1	61.9	39.9	74.1
5 p.m. - 8 p.m.	70.0	66.7	56.2	81.8	55.3	69.0

CSI Index

54.1	49.9	57.4	64.7	61.2	74.6
Period 1	Period 2	Period 3	Period 4	Period 5	Period 6

* *CSI is the average of Overall Satisfaction, Return, and Recommend.*

Alert report

Displays the results of a single survey, highlighting unacceptable answers that *triggered an alert* to be sent immediately to the unit manager. Integrated voice and text comments allow you to hear the *voice of the customer*. Additionally, there is an *incident management* section at the bottom for *follow-up accountability,* showing:

1. Local unit follow-up with customer, and
2. Internal action taken.

Alert

▶ = question(s) that generated alert

Survey Date: 07/23		**Location:** Restaurant 146	**Caller ID:** 555XXX8328
SATISFACTION RATINGS		SURVEY QUESTIONS	
Date of Service	**07/23**	Store Number	146
Survey Mode	**Phone**	Which day did we serve you?	Yesterday
Offer Code	**2261**	About how often do you dine with us?	Weekly
Employee ID	**173**	How likely are you to visit us again? ▶	Not Likely
Redemption Code	**1199**	Rate the service you received on your most recent visit.	Poor
		Based on your last response, we have some room for improvement. Where should we focus our attention?	Meal Pacing
		What was your main reason for choosing us?	Food Quality
		Were our employees attentive? ▶	No
		What additional services would you like us to provide?	(play .mp3 🔊)
		May we have a manager call you?	Yes
		Phone Number	555 XXX-8328
		Who should we ask for?	(play .mp3 🔊)

ACTION TAKEN (Follow-up Accountability)	
CLOSED	I called customer and discovered some of the staff were having a private conversation while helping the customer. As a result his service was slow. I 1) counseled staff, 2) explained to customer what I'd done. 3) Offered coupon for free dessert, he is satisfied. *Posted by Robert McAllister 07/23 3:02pm*
OPEN	Customer requests we call back. *Posted by System 07/23 12:32pm*

RESOLVED? ☑yes ☐no ☐in process

Analyzing the Data

Level Two Analysis

Basic Correlations and Regressions
(Please see "Analytical Tips and Tricks" at the end of this chapter for an important caution.)

These types of analyses are used to determine the strength and direction of relationships between two or more variables, and to determine <u>potential</u> "cause and effect" impacts between inputs and desired outcomes.

Example 1: Order accuracy has an extremely significant impact on "overall satisfaction" *(Visual correlation)*

Accuracy's Impact on Overall Satisfaction

"Overall Satisfaction" decreases significantly when the order is not accurate.

Example 2: Increase in service vs. increase in sales *(Statistical correlation)*

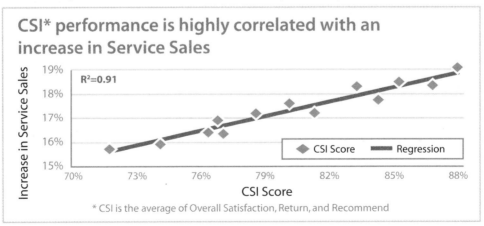

CSI* performance is highly correlated with an increase in Service Sales

$R^2=0.91$

* CSI is the average of Overall Satisfaction, Return, and Recommend

Key Driver Studies

Key driver analyses help discover what variables drive customers' willingness to recommend and/or to return (i.e., what is most important to driving their loyalty?). Performance against key drivers can be measured for the entire company or for individual units.

Example 1: Presenting stronger vs. weaker drivers

(i.e., variables most strongly correlated to "likelihood to recommend")

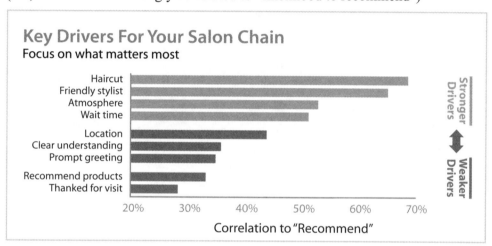

Example 2: Highlighting the operational "need areas" in a restaurant, by highlighting performance against key drivers

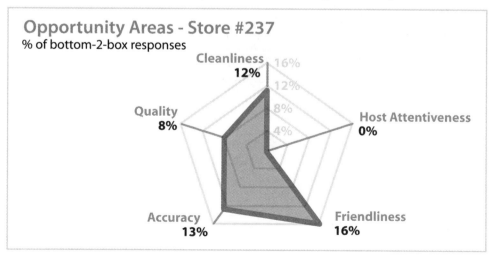

Benchmarking

Comparing results either internally across groupings, or externally across
competitors, etc.

Example 1: Benchmark comparison of "likelihood to recommend" across company regions

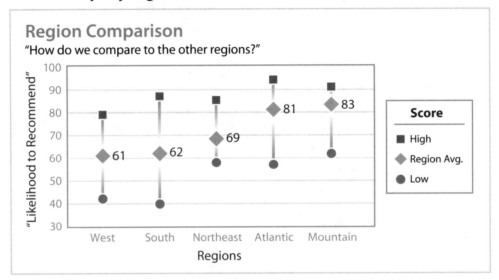

Example 2: Golf course benchmark comparison using two different scoring methods and detailing survey counts

Golf Course Benchmarking

Intent to return

Company	Scoring		Survey Detail	
	"Average" Method	"Top Box" Method	# of Surveys	% of Surveys
Course 1	94.7	84.6		
Course 2	93.0	81.7		
Course 3	93.6	80.2		
Course **XYZ**	**88.6**	**73.3**	10,250	15.2%
Course 5	89.6	72.5		
Course 6	89.3	72.1		
Course 7	83.0	59.8		
Course 8	78.0	46.1		
High	94.7	84.6		
Weighted Avg.	88.7	71.3	67,400	100.0%
Low	78.0	46.1		

Cross-tabs and filters

Filtering data based on specific combinations of variable inputs. Most often used to break down information into more granular parts *(e.g., how satisfied are first-time visitors compared to long-time customers?).*

Frequency of visits

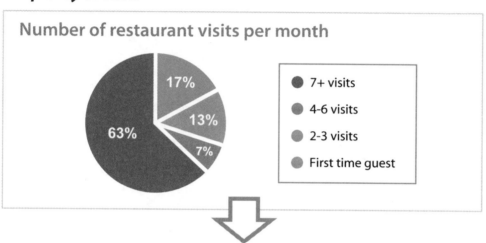

Further broken down to isolate levels of satisfaction by frequency of visit

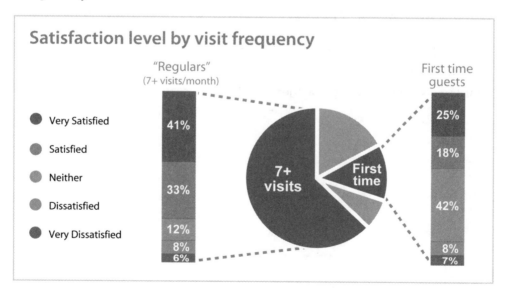

Analyzing the Data

Combination Presentations

Using single presentations to show multiple pieces of information.

Unit results, by variable, vs. benchmark vs. goals over time

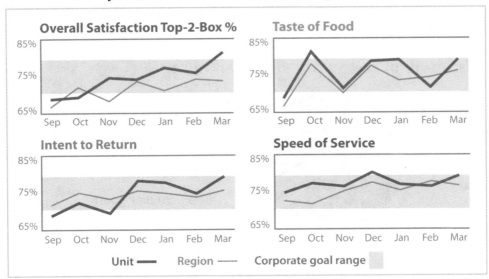

Satisfaction, by food delivery time and initial seating time

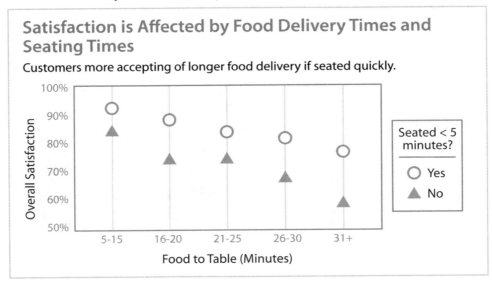

Benchmark range of performance, by call center, over time

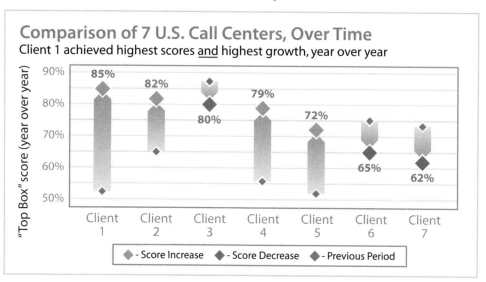

Comparison of 7 U.S. Call Centers, Over Time
Client 1 achieved highest scores <u>and</u> highest growth, year over year

Operational elements compared to each other, over time

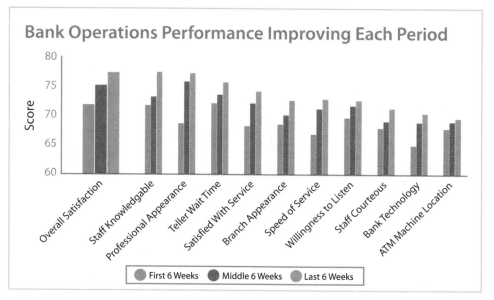

Bank Operations Performance Improving Each Period

Level Three Analysis

What I call "level three analysis" is comprised of important actionable findings that are discovered through a combination of more complex analyses, combined with deeper levels of experience in the analyst. Here are some examples:

Teasing out the "more subtle" nuances

Correlation showing that the key drivers in a client's bars are employee related, not product related. Effort should be focused on hiring "attitude" and less on making perfect drinks.

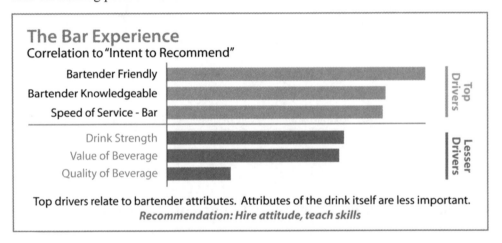

Graphical analysis showing menu preferences by geography. Highlights the need to vary appetizers across the country.

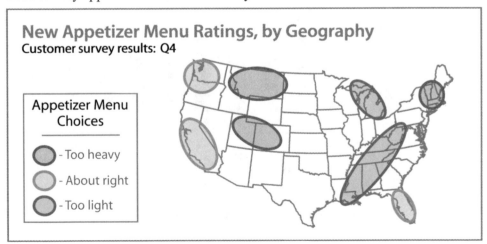

Causal Relationships

(Please see "Analytical Tips and Tricks" at the end of this chapter for an important caution)

Log-regression showing that as clients were asked, "Did your server recommend an add-on product?" sales of add-on products increased.

"Recommend Product" vs. Average Retail Sales Ticket

Regression showing that stores with highest CSI* also experienced the greatest increase in sales over time.

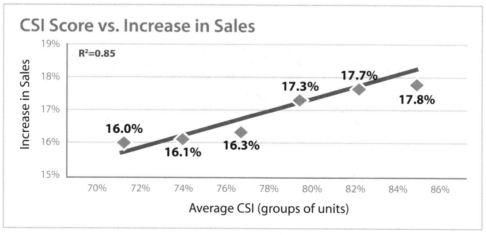

CSI Score vs. Increase in Sales

*Customer Satisfaction Index

More complex regressions, distributions, and multivariable combinations

Distinguishing "price-of-entry" services vs. "must have" services, penalty-reward contrast analysis, etc. Digging deeper to uncover more complex relationships.

Graphical representation of the lessening of variation in store performance over time. Variation is tightening, and overall scores are improving.

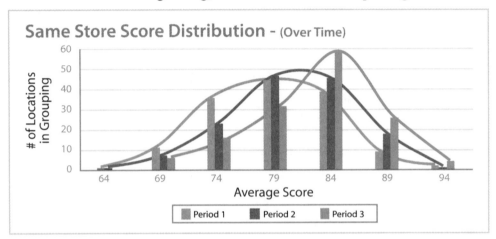

Comparing the joint effect of increasing service levels both in person and on the phone (i.e., the "total" is greater than the "sum-of-the-parts").

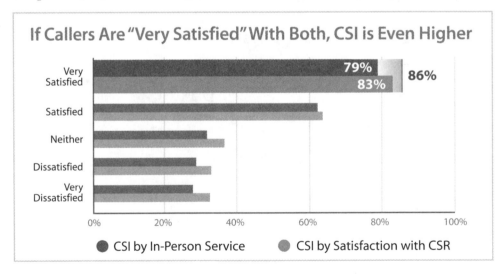

Penalty-reward-contrast analysis. Pinpoints areas that truly "delight" when done well compared to those that penalize when done poorly.

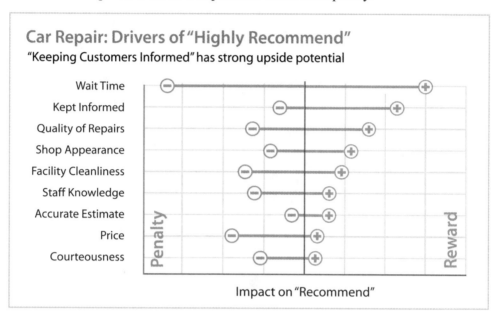

Car Repair: Drivers of "Highly Recommend"

"Keeping Customers Informed" has strong upside potential

Penalty

Reward

- Wait Time
- Kept Informed
- Quality of Repairs
- Shop Appearance
- Facility Cleanliness
- Staff Knowledge
- Accurate Estimate
- Price
- Courteousness

Impact on "Recommend"

Importance performance analysis (compound matrix). Compares "performance" vs. "importance" of key metrics – then, further demonstrates changes since last measurement date.

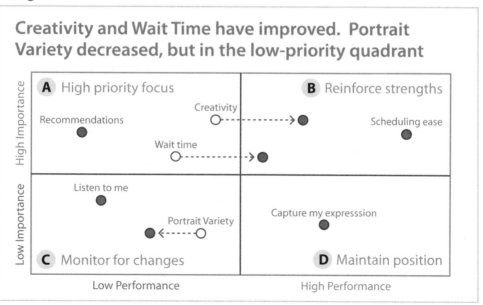

Creativity and Wait Time have improved. Portrait Variety decreased, but in the low-priority quadrant

A High priority focus

B Reinforce strengths

Recommendations

Creativity

Scheduling ease

Wait time

Listen to me

Portrait Variety

Capture my expresssion

C Monitor for changes

D Maintain position

High Importance

Low Importance

Low Performance

High Performance

Some Special Presentations

Occasionally circumstances call for more unique ways of presenting the data.

Speedometer chart
More eye-catching way of showing performance of several variables simultaneously (e.g., current year vs. last year, and vs. goals).

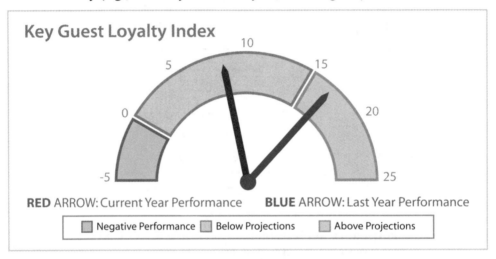

Bubble chart
Used to show 3-dimensions of data on a 2-dimensional graph.

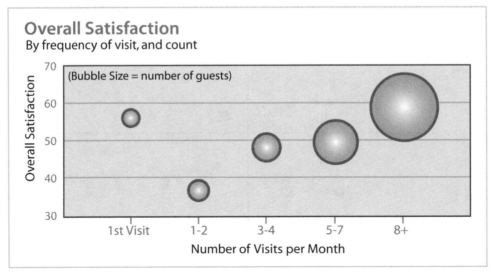

Panel chart

Comparing multiple units of the same time period without the clutter that would arise if all the lines were squeezed together.

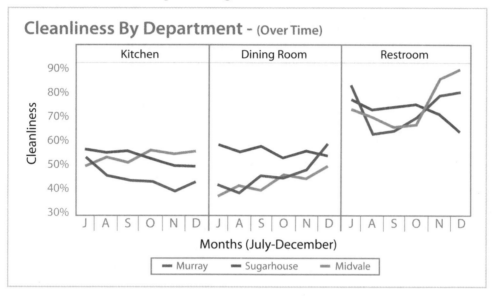

Radar chart

Used to quickly and visually pinpoint performance strengths and weaknesses across multiple variables, and across time.

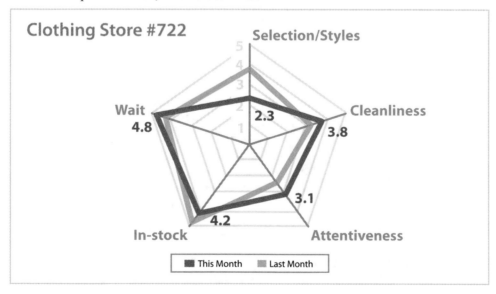

4. Some Analytical Tips and Tricks

Back-to-basics analysis

We've reviewed varying levels of analyses that can be used to measure and evaluate your company's performance and commitment to customer service. After covering the basics, I then presented some more advanced methods that are available, should a more sophisticated level of analysis be needed.

Now, let's return to the basics. Notwithstanding the complicated analytical tools available, most of the benefits from customer feedback analysis come from a few basic "list and trend" reports – (the old 80/20 rule in action: that is, 80% of the benefit comes from 20% of the tools). The reports and charts that provide the most value are those that answer these basic questions:

- Are we improving or declining?
- In which areas are we falling short over time?
- Are we responding to and following up on all service lapses?
- Which operational areas are the key drivers to an individual customer's loyalty and advocacy?
- How is store X performing vs. its peers? vs. its goals? vs. company averages? vs. best performers?
- How is employee Y performing against peers, goals, averages, and best performers?
- Which best practices can we share between stores?
- What customer suggestions can we develop further to improve our operations?

"Gentlemen, and Ladies, today we're going to get down to nuts and bolts..."

Always evaluate <u>both</u> absolute <u>and</u> time-based performance before judging

(Paying special attention to recent trends)

Let's look at an example of why it is important to always make sure any comparisons are prepared using both absolute *and* time-based measurements. The chart on the left could be used to graph the "up-selling" percentages of all the employees in a retail store. Absolute scores are compared to improvement over time. Employees scoring in quadrants C and D have below-average scores, and those in A and B have above-average scores. (These are our best performers.) But let's say that one of the employees has only been employed for a couple of weeks and is "learning the ropes." She is still scoring below average in up-selling, but she is really improving fast. She would not rank highly if we only looked at absolute score. However, on our matrix chart, she would show up in quadrant D, which is indicative of the **direction** of her improvement. Likewise, another employee could have a high absolute score, but be trending down over time. This is why both measurements need to be included.

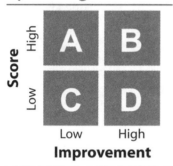

Up-Selling

Be aware of the difference between "percent" and "percentage points"

Here is an example of the pitfalls of not distinguishing between percentage changes and percentage point changes.

Difference Between "%" and "% Points"

Out of 200 possible points:

Score #1	Score #2
40 pts.	**50 pts.**

Absolute Difference:	**+10**	*(50 pts. minus 40 pts.)*
Percentage Difference:	**+25%**	*(10 pts./40 pts.)*
Percentage POINT Difference:	**+5% pts.**	*(20% to 25%)*

"Importance" – asked directly, or derived?

Satisfaction is not an absolute concept, it's a relative one. It is relative to what the customer thinks is important. When determining the key drivers of a customer's loyalty or satisfaction, the question that arises is this, "What is *important* to a customer? (We could put a couple of PhDs in a room and they might fight to the death on this question.) For our purposes, let me define an "important" attribute or action as one that causes the customer to be loyal, tell their friends, and/or return to buy more from you. The next question is how to *measure* importance – should we come right out and *ask them*, or should we *derive* the importance statistically by seeing which attributes most strongly impact the desired outcome? There have been studies supporting both methods. ***I generally encourage the use of the derived method.*** Let me briefly explain them both.

Direct method

There are lots of ways to ask a customer directly what they think is important. Here are three examples: (1) rate the variable using a scale from "not important" to "important," (2) rate the relative importance of pairs of attributes, and (3) give the customers 100 points and let them allocate points based on their perceived importance. *If* you are going to ask customers directly, I much prefer the latter rating method, because the allocation of a fixed number of points forces respondents to prioritize between choices.

Derived method

Rather than asking customers directly, I generally favor determining the "importance" of a service or product attribute *by deriving its importance statistically.* This is accomplished by estimating the impact that each potential predictor attribute has on the desired outcome. (For example, does the time it takes a phone representative to answer a question really impact a customer's decision to recommend that company to his or her friends?) Statistical estimations are more objective and less biased than direct methods.

The reason deriving importance is my preferred method is most easily explained using the old example of airline safety. If you *ask* customers to rank airline variables on importance, "safety" always wins. (Who could argue with the importance of safety relative to peanuts or schedules?) But when you *derive* key drivers statistically, safety rarely shows up. Why? Because it is assumed. (When customers get on an airplane, they expect it to arrive safely.)

While safety is clearly the number one concern of customers, it does not generally drive their satisfaction, their loyalty, or their choice of airline.

This leads us directly to another important tip, which is the mistake of avoiding key drivers (important things) altogether and spending effort and resources to fix unimportant attributes *just because they are low scoring.*

Don't confuse "low score" with "important low score"

Not all measurable variables contribute equally to rating the overall service experience or the potential to grow your business. An untrained analyst might mistakenly conclude that consistently low-rated items are where you should focus your efforts. In reality, the lowest-rated quality factors might just be the last place you should focus. Sometimes, variables with low scores have little to no relation to a customer's satisfaction or loyalty. However, you would never know this unless you statistically analyzed each survey question to determine its impact on an important outcome variable, such as "intent to recommend." (This is yet another reason for using a professional firm to assist you in your customer experience measurement.)

Here's a quick example: Have you ever heard anyone rant and rave about how delicious hospital food is? Neither have I. Therefore, it would probably not surprise you to know that "quality of the food" does not score very well in most hospital patient surveys. But guess what? It *also* barely makes the list of attributes correlated to a patient's "likelihood to recommend" a hospital. In other words, bad hospital food doesn't affect their loyalty. (i.e. they don't like the food, but it doesn't stop them from coming back or recommending a hospital to their friends.)

Best practice would suggest: (1) determining what your top "key drivers" are – those that most strongly impact the likelihood of a customer to recommend you, and then, (2) giving these areas the attention and the priority that will lead to an increase in your repeat business!

Positive correlation does not imply causality

Correlation and Causality. One common mistake made by people interpreting variable relationships is to assume that because two things are correlated, that one is *causing* the other.

Here is an example. I learned in Statistics 101 that research has found a positive correlation between:

Ice cream consumption, and:
- **Boating accidents**
- **Drownings**
- **Shark attacks**

If every correlation defined a causal relationship, then we would have to forbid eating ice cream due to the horrible things it causes. So, does ice cream consumption *cause* people to drown? No. The truth is that often two variables are related only *because of a third variable* that was not previously accounted for. In this example case, *the weather* is this third variable - because as the weather gets warmer, people tend to eat more ice cream. Warmer weather also results in an increase in swimming and boating, and therefore increased drownings, boating accidents, and shark attacks. So, when evaluating variable relationships, be sure to recognize that the variables may be *related,* but their relationship does not necessarily mean that the change in one *causes* the change in the other.

Don't manage to "exceptions"

As managers begin to receive detailed and relevant feedback from their customers, there is sometimes a tendency to do a knee-jerk reaction to individual or small groups of data. May I suggest the following:

DON'T
- Fire an employee for one or two bad surveys. (Generally.)
- Close a store because the fish was greasy one night.
- Stop collecting customer feedback because of a few "fat-fingered" or mistaken survey responses.
- Do *anything* based on a few data points.

DO
- Evaluate trends over time.
- Confirm issues using several sources, if possible.
- Dig into the root causes of issues.
- Watch for emerging trends.

"Why are all these dots red?"

5. Scoring Options for Survey Data

There are many different scoring options to choose from. They vary in complexity in both calculation and in use, and each method has pros and cons. In the table that follows, I use a simple range of 1 to 5 (5 being the highest) to introduce several of the most common scoring methods used in measuring the customer experience. The table shows four <u>example</u> methods. (There are many more to choose from.)

The first is the **<u>Average</u>** scoring method. Each of the five answers is given a set of points to be awarded. In this case, I am showing a simple 0 to 100 scale using 25-point intervals. (You might alternatively choose a weighted average version using derived importance weights.) Two columns to the right is the **<u>Top Box</u>** scoring method, which says that "anything less than perfection" is a zero. People who use this method also like to say things like, "Close only counts in horseshoes and hand grenades."* (Another variation of this method is the Top-Two-Box score, where both a "4" and a "5" would be given full score.) Between these two is a **<u>Hybrid</u>** method, which assigns points in declining scale to only the Top Three Box answers. Other methods for scoring include creating a **<u>Net</u>** score where lower scores are subtracted from higher scores (one example is shown below). The most well known presentation of this type of net scoring was introduced by Frederick Reichheld.**

Note that even though the underlying survey responses are identical, the "Total Score" varies significantly for each scoring method (from 77 to 48).

Scoring Options

Same survey answers - different scores (examples only)

	Raw Survey Responses	Average Score	Hybrid Score	Top Box Score	Net Score
Excellent - 5	54	100	100	54	54
Good - 4	20	75	50	0	0
Average - 3	12	50	25	0	0
Fair - 2	8	25	0	0	0
Poor - 1	6	0	0	0	(-6)
Total	**100**	Score **77**	**67**	**54**	**48**

Conservative ⬅➡ Aggressive

* *(Attributed to Frank Robinson)*

** *("The One Number You Need to Grow," by Frederick Reichheld, Harvard Business Review, Dec 2003.)*

> ### Special note on aggressive scoring methods
>
> When an aggressive scoring method is used, it is often used to score the "will you recommend?" question, and sometimes the researcher will suggest asking only that single question. I *agree* that in many cases, using an aggressive scoring method is a very good way to distinguish between true advocates of your brand and those who are neutral or negative. I generally *agree* that the "will you recommend?" question is one of, if not *the* most important questions to ask on a survey. I generally *disagree* that it is the *only* quantitative question that should be asked on a survey. (For a more detailed discussion on this, see the chapter titled, "Take no shortcuts," page 35.)   Beyond just the mathematical differences in different scoring methods, let's now consider some of the other pros and cons of using an aggressive scoring method.

Aggressive scoring methods have pros and cons that need to be considered. Before choosing an aggressive scoring method, you should carefully consider the following:

▬ Simplicity

Simple averages are more easily explained and dissected. Some aggressive scoring methods are more complex and can't be easily dissected or understood by local unit operators.

✚ Higher Standard Setting

Aggressive scoring methods differentiate true "evangelist customers" from the merely "satisfied." Companies using aggressive scoring methods recognize the power in "extremely satisfied" customers, and hold the bar higher for expectations of local operators. Those using aggressive scoring recognize that loyalty rises exponentially and not linearly – in other words, a "5" customer is substantially more loyal than a "4," and therefore worth a lot more to your company.

▬ Morale

Aggressive scoring methods have significantly lower resultant scores. (Employees accustomed to scoring in the 80s and 90s may be shocked to see a customer satisfaction score of 45.) Absolute standards such as 90 = "A," 80 = "B," and 70 = "C" may cause significant morale issues with people who have been accustomed from grade school to college with standard school grading methods. So, if you are going to use an aggressive scoring method, like Top-Box, Top-Two-Box, Net Scoring, or others, then you must: (1) over-communicate, and (2) grade on a "curve." It has also been my experience that, after a shift to an aggressive scoring method, a number of store or franchise managers will begin to whine and complain and "blame everything that moves" as to why their scores have dropped. Prepare for this in advance.

✚ *Tightness of the performance of units being measured*

On the other hand, to use an over-worn cliché, aggressive scoring methods really "separate the men from the boys." You may be one of the blessed companies in your industry for whom everything seems to fall into place. Customers love you. Customers love your products. All of your retail locations and call center representatives average over 90% satisfaction rating! Lucky you. In such a case, an aggressive scoring method is just what is needed to separate the pack. The focus moves quickly to "perfection" rather than "averages," and only the very strongest performers stay at the top of the pack. In this case, an aggressive scoring method can differentiate your true "advocate customers" from the merely "satisfied."

▬ *Lack of details*

Aggressive methods of scoring make it very difficult to review the details and distribution of the answer sets. Because the details are not presented, we are unable to evaluate the full range of answers. For example, how many "satisfied" are there? How many "very poor" experiences are there? With some aggressive methods there is the additional problem of explaining the number itself. For example, when some surveys are netted against others, it is possible to arrive at a resultant final score in multiple ways. For example, 65% top scores less 35% bottom scores results in a net score of 30%. But so does 50% less 20%. Completely different situations can result in the same "net" score.

A final consideration – *actionability*

To reiterate a point I made in an earlier chapter, some consultants commingle the decision on scoring methodology with how *many questions* should be asked on the survey itself. Remember, surveys that ask only a few questions often leave you with very little actionable information. You may end up calculating a "final score," but you may not know what *corrective action* steps are required for you to improve.

So what is the "right" scoring method to use to measure the customer experience? **There is no single best method.** However, here are my recommendations.

Baseline Scoring Method Recommendation:

1. I suggest that you begin with the ***average*** scoring method (either weighted or unweighted).

2. Combine multiple general metrics to arrive at a ***composite score***, such as customer satisfaction index, or CSI. (CSI = an average of overall satisfaction, likelihood to return, and intent to recommend.) The reason for this is as follows: although "likelihood to recommend" has been shown to be the best predictor of financial success in many cases, there may be a large number of customers who are thrilled with their experience, but would not "recommend" any service to anyone. (They're just not "recommenders.") Additionally, individual metrics more easily "bounce up and down," while a combination of several metrics remains more stable over time. For these reasons, I suggest combining the three questions above into a score to act as the ultimate "target."

3. Over time, if you are not seeing enough ***differentiation*** between unit performance, then consider changing to a more aggressive method.

4. Before making the change to a more aggressive method, determine if your company culture can handle the ***morale issues*** potentially caused by the lower scores (i.e., you wouldn't want to make the change to an aggressive method, and then have your CEO rake someone over the coals for a low score).

5. ***Communicate*** like crazy – before you make the change, and during the transition.

6. Use specific questions to generate understanding and to provide actionable ***diagnosis of root causes*** and opportunities for improvement.

NOTE: *I like to present results using two or three scoring methods side-by-side for a few months so executives will become accustomed to the differences between conservative and aggressive scoring methods. As of this writing, approximately 50% of my clients are using average scoring, and the others are using one of the more aggressive methods of scoring.*

Part V

Using Customer Feedback to Improve

Speed and responsiveness

"Do it! Do it now!" (Spencer W. Kimball)

Nothing speaks volumes like <u>urgency</u>!

Another best practice in dealing with customers involves the overwhelming uniqueness of *speed of response.* At this point in my life, for certain professions (like house contractors, appliance repair, cable TV installation, etc.), I have already surrendered and lowered my expectations to: *"Please, just show up within an hour of your appointment and I'll be happy!"* Imagine how much word-of-mouth business a carpenter or home repairman would have if they had the authentic reputation of showing up, on time, when they said they would be there.

I believe *speed* and *urgency* are among the most powerful differentiators in business!

Urgency is an attitude, an approach to excellence. It doesn't mean being harried or chaotic or out of control – it does mean being fully engaged. When he was a young man, my dad worked at a soda fountain. He loved to tell us stories about when he was the only one behind the counter and how fast he could serve people. As a kid, whenever I had to stand in a line with my dad, we would carefully watch the servers and I quickly came to learn the meaning of the term "sense of urgency." Another example of urgency occurs during football season. Football teams accomplish miracles during the last two minutes of a game. Why not play with that intensity and attitude for the entire game?

A similar thing happens right before holidays and just before 'finals week' for a college student. We suddenly get more organized, we make checklists, and use our time more efficiently.

Urgency says, "I've seen the game films, now I want to go out and hit somebody!"

People who radiate urgency complete tasks <u>ahead</u> of deadlines. I had a colleague that would always quote...

"If I really wanted it today, I would have asked for it tomorrow!"

One of our clients provides food for major sporting stadiums across the U.S. During a baseball game at Wrigley Field, a customer had ordered chicken strips to be delivered directly to her suite. When the food arrived, the chicken strips were cold. She had also received an invitation to take a survey, providing feedback on her experience. She called right away and complained about the cold food. Instantly, the manager received a notification on his cell phone. He went directly to his computer and pulled up this customer's information from the system. *Before the game was over*, he found the upset customer, apologized, and presented her with some fresh, hot chicken strips. The customer was *blown away* at such responsiveness. Every day, companies have the opportunity to "wow" their customers by inviting them to provide feedback and then responding with urgency.

Sales forces in conference rooms around the world are trying their best to come up with value-adds that will take the pressure off of price and help them close sales. But, they often are missing the solution right under their nose: **strong relationships, fostered by speed, responsive service, and urgency, make price almost irrelevant.**

"Would you like that done soon,
pretty soon, or sometime-or-other?"

PRACTICAL TACTICS: (Questions to ponder)

How fast do you respond? Do your customers sense urgency in your employees' attitudes and actions?

Operations improvement through customer involvement

"I caught the bus - now what do I do with it?"

So, now what are you going to *do* with all of this feedback?

The answer comes to us from Sir Winston Churchill who had a favorite note he'd pen on documents that would come across his desk:

> ## "Action. This Day!"

I have to admit, the most frustrating part of working with hundreds of companies on customer experience measurement is when I occasionally have a client who is doing everything "right" but still not getting positive results. They are diligently measuring customer feedback, steadily increasing their scores, and communicating results throughout the organization, but the company's financial performance continues to deteriorate and customers are still defecting.

When this happens, some internal murmuring starts, senior management begins to question the efficacy of gathering customer feedback at all, and I get a phone call from the CEO questioning how this could be so.

After a brief analysis of the circumstances, nine times out of ten, I discover the following situation:

The company has been conscientious in its effort to *measure* satisfaction. They have been completely committed to obtaining and *communicating* results. But, they have had *no commitment to improving* the level of service; no follow up on needed training, no inclusion of customer satisfaction results in bonus plans, and no one has been held accountable for following up with and recovering customers who complained about a service lapse. It's incredible. They will collect the customer feedback. They will listen with both ears. They will hear positives, negatives, and suggestions. And then they will just sit there and do… **nothing**. This then fuels a downward spiral, where dissatisfied customers never return, leaving a diminishing customer base, with a higher proportion of easy-to-please customers and therefore, an increase in satisfaction scores. Particularly disappointing are those companies or managers who say something like, "Well, we're doing pretty well so far, why do we need to change?" (Just remember what the man who jumped off the Empire State Building said as he passed the 40th floor on his way down…"So far, so good!")

Success requires *action* and *commitment!* You must take action. You can't sit still. Let me quote a client's customer who says it more forcefully:

> ## "Why should I spend my time giving you feedback, when you didn't pay attention to my comments the last time?"
>
> *(Actual customer comment)*

Communicate and Measure!

One of the most important keys to continuous improvement is the need to institutionalize customer measurement. The best way I know to do that is to communicate, communicate, communicate! This can be through sophisticated

means, such as formal review processes and large performance systems, or as simple as a "back office bulletin board" (See example at right). The important thing is to clearly set high expectations among the employees and then hold them accountable for delivering at a superior level. Best results come from employee involvement in developing and executing against improvement action plans.

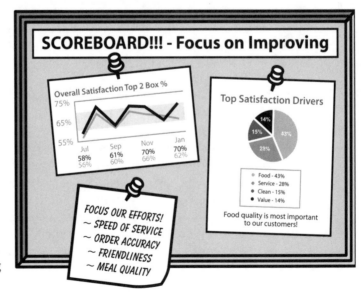

Action Steps:

Here's a quick summary list of *action steps* to take, now that you have committed to collect the customer experience data, learn from it, and improve. You may want to use this list in your internal discussions.

☐ **Collect and listen to customers' input**

☐ **Establish the process**
- Establish a standard schedule (at all management levels) to review the feedback.
- Focus on under- and over-performing units, teams, and associates.

☐ **Share and standardize best practices**
- Communicate the learnings.
- Set goals for improvement and emulation.
- Hold people accountable.
- Team up high performers with low performers.

☐ **Train and support your employees**
- Teach how to do the job and how to exceed expectations.
- Train how to really connect with customers.
- Equip employees/units with appropriate tools.

☐ **Reward and counsel**
- Reward in public, counsel in private.
- Reward both correct and improving behavior.
- Counsel those who cannot or will not improve.

☐ **Make the needed changes**
- Empower local managers to take action.
- Fix problems.
- Focus on what is working and expand it.

☐ **Show the customer the changes**

☐ **Repeat**

In the details

Pay attention to the details; your customers do

I started to write this chapter about paying attention to details, and I found an interesting thing about the old cliché that ends with the words, "...in the details." Depending upon where you grew up, the saying is quoted as either God is in the details, or the Devil is in the details. Anyway, I've decided to create my own version:

"The customer is in the details."

Jan Carlzon, the former president of Scandinavian Airlines, wrote a book called, *Moments of Truth.** (I'm told the term was borrowed from the "momento de verdad" in the Spanish bullring when the matador and the bull face each other.) Carlzon described a moment of truth as any time that a customer comes into contact with any aspect of a business. Speaking of Scandinavian Airlines, he said:

> ### "SAS is 'created' 50 million times a year, 15 seconds at a time. These 50 million 'moments of truth' are the moments that ultimately determine whether SAS will succeed or fail as a company."*

Carlzon used this concept in his turnaround efforts. Here is a partial list of moments of truth in the airline industry (to help you get started thinking about your industry):

Airline moments of truth (examples)

- Make a *reservation* (phone, web, in person)
- *Check bags* (curbside or inside)
- Baggage handler *attitude*
- Get a *ticket*
- Go through *security*
- *Greeted* at the gate
- *Seated* on the plane
- Provided *delicious peanuts*
- Charged to watch a *movie*
- Retrieve *luggage*, etc.

* (See "Moments of Truth," by J. Carlzon, Ballinger Publishing, 1987.)

In effect, what Carlzon said with his understanding of moments of truth, is that it is ***the details*** that make or break successful companies. All industries have moments of truth and *almost all moments of truth involve people!* So, what are the best practices of companies that "get this?" Here are a few formal and informal company policies to get your ideas flowing about the way you are, or are not, handling details at your company:

- The answer is "yes," now what was your question?
- "That's not my job" does not exist at our company.
- We answer e-mails in this order:
          (1) customers, (2) family, (3) personal
- We will call all customers back within five minutes.
- Our only success is a returning customer.
- If it's not our fault, it's still our problem.
- Our employees don't consider this only a "job."
- All employees are empowered to "make it right."
- In all we do, we run through and beyond the finish line.
- We are always improving. Success is never final.
- "Lagniappe" *(above and beyond)* is in our blood!
- Our customers' perception *is* their reality.

"Ready. Set. CLOSE!"

How important are details?

I walked up to a pizza store once at 9:59 pm – closing time. Guess what happened? The young lady *raced me to the door* from inside. She got to the door first, turned the lock, then flipped over the "Closed" sign. We were literally six inches apart, except for the glass door! She mouthed the words, "I have a date." There was no, "Sorry for the inconvenience." There was no recognition that I am the money-paying reason that she is even employed. There wasn't even a smile! I've never been back.

Has something like this happened to you before? Wow, what a miserable moment of truth for them. I've told that pizza-store story over a hundred times! This is the *worst* kind of marketing for a company!

Compare my pizza story with the Ritz-Carlton housekeeper who is taught to drop whatever she is doing and walk you to the restaurant if you happen to ask her where it is. Ritz-Carlton's service attitude creates the *very best* type of marketing, which is a happy customer with a big mouth! And, the best way to gain one of these is *by jumping into the details*.

What are your individual customer touch points?

Are you paying attention to the details?

Do you have a tool in place to measure your "moments of truth?"

PRACTICAL TACTICS: (Questions to ponder)

What are the "moments of truth" for your company and for your industry? Have you mapped them out? Do you have a required performance standard for each moment of truth? Do employees know what's expected of them? How are you performing against your standard?

Reducing internal variation

"We have met the enemy and he is us!"   (Walt Kelly)

It's not enough to just be better than the competition, You've got to be better than yourself!*

Even though you are better than your competitors, you are probably still killing yourself with the ***variation between your locations*** or your employee groups. It has been said,

"There is less to fear from outside competition than there is to fear from *internal* inefficiency, discourtesy, and bad service."

(Anonymous)

Do you remember the old joke about the two guys being chased by a bear through the forest? The one guy stops to put on his tennis shoes, and his friend says, "Don't be stupid. You can't outrun a bear!" To which the first responds, "I don't have to outrun the bear. I only have to outrun you!"

I worry that we've taken the principle behind this joke too far in our daily business lives. Somehow, we got the notion over the last few decades, that success is simply a function of beating the other guy. But this can't be the only measure of success we use. What if the other guy is mediocre? Then we're only better than the "bottom of the barrel." What words do they put on your award for beating mediocre?

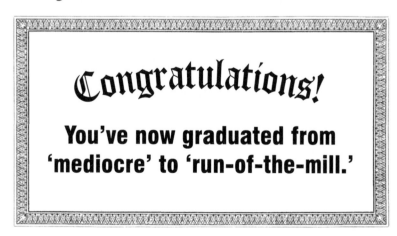

Congratulations!

You've now graduated from 'mediocre' to 'run-of-the-mill.'

* *(Adapted from William Faulkner)*

Reducing Internal Variation

Occasionally, CEOs will call me to discuss a pressing issue. Once in a while, our conversation will proceed something along these lines:

Client: I can't understand why I need to continue measuring our customers' experience. We are significantly better than any of our competitors, and we have been steadily increasing the gap between us each year.

Me: But there is always room for improvement, right?

Client: That's true, but the *average score* across all of our stores is 94%. Doesn't that mean that we are already approaching our best?

Me: Possibly, except for one small fact, which is this:

> *"...the variations within a company easily dwarf the differences between competitors!"* *

"Customers experience variation, not averages!"*

Two of my favorite anonymous sayings, tailor-made for this issue, are these:

> **"Don't quote statistics to me. I've been in a statistics factory and I know how they're made."**

> **"If I put my head in the oven, and my feet in the freezer, on average, I'm warm!**
>
> **Averages lie!"**

(Both quotes from "Manage Your Human Sigma" by Fleming, Coffman, Harter, Harvard Business Review, July 2005.)

It isn't enough to measure high-level averages – you need to measure *individual customers* dealing with *individual employees,* and drive for…

CONSISTENCY! CONSISTENCY! CONSISTENCY!

Exceptional companies know that they aren't just battling their competitors. They know that they aren't just battling against best practices in other industries. They know that their biggest battle is against inconsistency, apathy, and the weakest spots in their own internal front-line employees or outlets. I recently spoke at a national franchise meeting of one of the country's biggest and most-recognizable restaurant chains. I showed the graph below, and then played a voice message that one of their customers left on a feedback survey. The customer does a better job than I could of illustrating the dangerous outcome of inconsistency:

"You really have great restaurants, and we especially like your _____ store. Here's the thing though – *we drive past two of your other stores* to get to that one, because the employees are so much better at that location."

(Actual customer comment)

One Company's Inconsistent Execution
Customer Satisfaction between stores in the United Kingdom

Listen to this commentary from the same *Harvard Business Review* referenced earlier.

> **"High-level averages of company performance may provide good marketing copy, and they may make executives feel better about their position in the marketplace. But because they obscure the considerable *variation from location to location within a company*, they don't give managers and executives the information they need to improve performance."***

> **"...the variations _within_ a company easily dwarf the differences between competitors!" ***

Those two quotes are worth reading again. Would you please?

Maybe it's time to stop worrying so much about the "other guys," and start worrying more about the *variation* between your own locations and employees. Make internal inconsistency "Enemy #1."

The quality of
your experience
with our company
DEPENDS
on which store
you go to!

PRACTICAL TACTICS: (Questions to ponder)

Create a list (or bar chart) of your locations, franchisees, teams, associates, etc. and rank them from high to low. What is the gap between the best and worst? Set a clear standard of performance and a date when it will no longer be acceptable to be below standard. Start thinning out the bottom 10%. Ask members of the top 20% to mentor the bottom 20%.

---

* *(From "Manage Your Human Sigma," Fleming et al., Harvard Business Review, July 2005.)*

Utilizing positive feedback

"Thank you for the compliment"

Motivating employees through positive feedback!
("But dad, what about the five 'A's?")

The sub-title for this chapter comes from a story that my father used to tell about the young man who showed his report card to his dad. The father, noticing a "C+" in social studies, started to chastise the boy. To which the young man responded, "But dad, what about the five 'A's'?"

We all work in industries that can be very critical at times. We are all focused on improving. Our desire to improve necessitates using a critical eye to find problems. It is easy to slip into the trap of focusing solely on the negative aspects of our service and product delivery. Picking ourselves up when we fall. Improving in areas where we are weak. Focusing on fixing the problems.

But, this overlooks the other half of the equation, which is the **positive** customer and employee feedback that can be used to *motivate, instill passion, reward, and recognize.*

A touching memory

Let me tell you about an extremely poignant memory. I was the keynote speaker at the national franchise convention of one of the large salon chains. I had prepared what I thought was a great speech, replete with charts, graphs, analytics, and all of the requisite slides. The analysis that the Mindshare team had produced was exceptional, and even better, the result of measuring the customers' experience for 12 months was strongly-improved customer satisfaction, and a statistically verified 7% increase in sales! But, very little of the statistics remain with me in memory.

What I do remember occurred just 10 minutes before I was scheduled to go on stage, when one of the biggest franchisees approached me during a break and asked if I would be willing to play a customer voice comment that had been captured about one of his employees. I quickly added the comment to my presentation, and at the appropriate time invited a very frightened young lady to join me on the stage while I played the customer's extremely complimentary comments about her in front of about a thousand people (including her supervisors, all the way up the franchise company's organization chart). The customer's comments were not only about the haircut, but also about the kindness and empathy she had shown to this customer during a difficult time in his life.

There was not a dry eye in the house. After she was escorted from the room (to a standing ovation), I remarked to the crowd that, certainly this was a day she'd never forget, and that we probably wouldn't see her name on the employee turnover sheet anytime soon. In fact, at each conference over the next few years, she made it a point to come up and share a smile with me.

Nothing beats the power of positive reinforcement! Nothing!

One of the most important reports we create for our clients is the "Exceptional Service Report." This report singles out instances of exceptional service by locations and by employees. I love it. It gives everyone a short vacation from "continuous improvement" in order to celebrate successful activities, and even more importantly, successful *people.* Here are a couple of tips you might want to consider:

1. Make it a big deal to *"catch your employees"* doing good things.
2. Praise them for it *in public*.
3. Give them an *unexpected reward* occasionally, to show them how important they are to the organization.

"Every human being is trying to say something to others. Trying to cry out, 'I am alive, notice me! Speak to me! Confirm that I am important, that I matter!'"
(Marion D. Hanks)

PRACTICAL TACTICS: (Questions to ponder)

How can you use customer feedback to praise and reward your employees? What positive reinforcement programs do you have in place? Who and when was the last employee you personally complimented on doing a good job?

The balanced scorecard

Long-term thinking with multiple metrics

Historical measures of company success

Financial metrics have been the main scorecard of a company's success for hundreds of years. But by themselves, they don't tell the story of how a business is performing. Financials measure what has *already happened* – the past. That works fine when things don't change much. But someone has said that with today's accelerating pace, running a company using financial data alone is like driving down the highway using only the rear-view mirror.

Additionally, financial metrics do a great job of valuing *tangible assets*. But today, *intangible assets* such as quality, responsiveness, motivation, customer loyalty, learning capability, and employee loyalty that are often more important than physical assets. Yet traditional financial accounting generally only considers physical assets.

Short-term vs. Long-term thinking

If you hold a manager accountable only for financial measures, you may increase profits in the short term, but you're probably going to hurt the company in the long run. Unfortunately, the focus of most public companies is necessarily short-term – i.e., making more money today. It is not uncommon to hear CEOs of public companies complain about their need to make stupid short-term decisions in order to meet the public's need for quarterly dividends or increasing earnings. In order to meet these constraints, some may reduce staff, sacrifice quality, or cut research, training, or advertising, all of which impair the long-term success of the company. (For example, companies that cut advertising expenses during a recession seem to have a more difficult recovery than those that maintained those expenditures.)

Another example involves short-sighted thinking on employment practices. I monitored the hotel industry through a couple of low points, and I watched in disbelief while some more short-term-minded franchisees would try to cut back on needed restaurant staff or on housekeepers in order to save money. Invariably, such short-term decisions can lead to long-term problems in making future profits.

What is needed is a way to use metrics from each of the main drivers in a company to measure the overall health of a business.

Introducing the balanced scorecard*

The balanced scorecard, formalized by Kaplan and Norton in 1992, is a simple concept (executed in many different ways), that has at its core the goal to use a balanced set of metrics to measure the health of a business. In practicality, this means expanding management's view beyond the financial metrics and adding other metrics to balance out the equation.

The balanced scorecard is a subject replete with pamphlets, books, and websites, all devoted to teaching you its subtleties, nuances, and proper implementation. (I'll leave it to you, your search engine, and your consulting budget to decide how much more detailed information you'd like. I would, however, strongly recommend you read the writings of Kaplan and Norton.) What I'd like to do here is to introduce the basics of the balanced scorecard in the form and structure that makes the most sense to me.

The four areas addressed in the original presentation of the balanced scorecard were:

- **Financial Perspective** – How is your organization performing financially? What financial metrics are the key indicators of success?
- **Customer Perspective** – How do your customers perceive your company? How can you best understand the loyalty of your customers across the various touch points in your organization?
- **Internal Business Perspective** – What must your company excel at? How successful is the execution of your company's key business processes? What metrics best indicate both efficient and effective performance?
- **Innovation and Learning Perspective** –What elements in your organization most contribute to your company's ability to innovate, improve, and learn?

Since the original work was published, consultants and business leaders have suggested additional measurement areas and supplied alternative titles for some of the original four areas. The balanced scorecard has evolved and adapted.

(See "The Balanced Scorecard: Measures that Drive Performance," by Robert S. Kaplan and David P. Norton, Harvard Business Review, January 1992.)

For example, I know of one company that chooses to measure the following five areas:

- Financial results
- Customer satisfaction
- Employee satisfaction
- Internal efficiency
- Competitive results

> *"Guest satisfaction scores are now an integral part of how we are rewarding our managers."*
>
> Client

Adding in the specifics

To me, the clearest presentation of the balanced scorecard is shown in a table format with the key measurement areas listed across the top, followed by a list of measurable variables, then targets, and finally initiatives.

For example, for "Customer" we might present a column of information as follows:

Perspective:	Customer
Metric:	Customer Satisfaction
Measurable Variables:	(CSI) customer satisfaction index
Target:	93% CSI (+2% vs. last year)
Initiatives:	(1) Order accuracy, (2) reduced wait times, (3) 100% customer follow-up

While designing a complete balanced scorecard is outside the scope of this brief introduction, I would suggest that when you create yours, you include key measurement areas that *tie to strategic objectives* of your company and that you can *continuously measure*. I hope customer and employee satisfaction will be on your list.

Compensation: An uncanny stumbling block!

I have found that the one area of the balanced scorecard that continues to elude many executives is arguably the single most important element to its implementation – compensation. Many executives understand the concepts of the balanced scorecard. They get fired up about getting it implemented in their company. They spend time choosing the right key metrics and measurable variables. But then, they never add the "mojo." They never put in the "nose ring" – they never change their reward systems! Almost every company I approach tells me they use a balanced scorecard to run their business. Then I ask this simple question:

"Are your managers being <u>bonused</u> on customer and employee satisfaction/loyalty?"

The answer is quite often, "Well, uhh, no." (Isn't it amazing, how one simple question can clarify an issue?)

You see, I believe that very little of this will make a difference unless your executives, your managers, your employees, and your whole company are all aligned together toward the same measurable goals. A scorecard is not balanced if it measures each of the areas, but doesn't incorporate them in compensation. It isn't balanced if the manager's bonus is calculated only by comparison to prior-year financials or comparison to a financial budget that was created in the dark dungeons of "corporate headquarters" months ago!

Here's a slight adaptation to an earlier aphorism I presented:

"That which gets measured *and <u>rewarded</u> gets done!*"*

Rewards are *the* way for a company to put its money where its mouth is!

May I suggest that you...

☑ ***Learn about the balanced scorecard***
☑ ***Adopt it***
☑ ***Infuse it into your culture***
☑ ***Incorporate it into your managers' bonuses***
☑ ***Measure each area zealously***

PRACTICAL TACTICS: (Questions to ponder)

How do you measure business success? How do you bonus your managers? Are you still focused only on short-term financial results? Or, have you expanded to include at least customer satisfaction and hopefully employee satisfaction into your standard metrics?

---

* (Anonymous. Popularized by Gordon Bethune and others.)

Using customer feedback for marketing

Customers "pitching" customers

One of the greatest side benefits of capturing the voice of the customer is your ability to use that information to: (1) test new ideas on real customers, and (2) enhance your marketing programs.

Customers helping with market research

The introduction of "New Coke"* is an interesting case study in the intersection between customer feedback and marketing. Coke is one of the best-known products in the world. In 1985, Coca-Cola decided to change the original recipe of Coke and create a new product. The marketing attracted lots of customers, but the drink itself was not well accepted. Management was inundated with customers complaining about the change. They listened, quickly responded, and within months, "New Coke" was off the shelves and the company went back to the old formula.

"Our study concludes that this is the percentage of our customers who will buy from us without any effort whatsoever on our part."

The company avoided a lot of financial repercussions by responding quickly. However, if management had initially listened more carefully to their loyal customers, they might have saved a lot of effort. Similarly, your existing customers can usually tell you right away if a new product or service offering is going to succeed.

The truth is that the best marketing tools you have available are not the brilliant minds working in your marketing department or the market research firms that are paid so much to analyze and investigate. Your best marketing tools are your *current customers* who visit your business every day. They know your strengths and weaknesses personally.

* (Coke and Coca Cola are trademarks of the Coca-Cola Company.)

A great source of marketing ideas

By engaging your customers in surveys that capture their true feelings, you can arm yourself with real-time information to help you improve your marketing. There is no reason to start from scratch every time you want to create a new marketing message. Why not let your current customers brag on you? The key to real-time customer feedback systems is that they give you integrated qualitative and quantitative feedback **immediately after** the service experience. No matter how many focus groups or demographic surveys you do, none of them will be as useful as getting candid opinions from someone who just had an experience with your products or service.

Here are a just a few example ways that customer feedback has been used in marketing efforts.

General "positive spin" statistics

You've seen these ads all over the place. Quality awards for new cars. On-time airplane arrivals. "Why customers are switching to us?" Gather the data from your customers and/or outside entities and use it to your benefit.

Testimonials

One of the best sources of material are the verbatim verbal or text comments collected from customers during surveys. These quotes, captured in the customer's own voice and style, often provide rich information, including testimonials that can be placed right into a marketing campaign. A widely-used example of this is from insurance companies who often share short success stories customers have had with them.

Customer suggestions

"You asked us for more (appetizers, cupholders, variety). We delivered!"

Specific strengths

One idea that has worked well over the years is to quote specific strengths. If your customers tell you that you're really great at something, consider using that message in your marketing. Let's say you continually receive positive feedback about the responsiveness of your staff; why not share it in your advertising? Some of the greatest marketing campaigns have stemmed from overwhelmingly positive survey feedback – remember this one: "Four out of five dentists agree?"

Fix a problem and then tell the story

Another way to make use of customer feedback is to clear up problems in your services or products, and then use marketing to get the message out that "you heard" what your customers told you. Understand your weaknesses, fix your operations, and turn them into positives. Then tell the world about the changes you've made. A more recent example of this are those restaurant chains who quickly switched away from unhealthy trans-fats after receiving numerous complaints from their customers. Those chains that acted quickly to remove these unhealthy oils got some "public image points" because of their quick and direct response.

Internal marketing

You should also use customer feedback for internal marketing. Use positive feedback to publicly encourage staff (e.g. posters, awards, etc.), while negatives can be used for private training and counseling purposes.

How to spread the word

After gathering information from your customers' feedback, you can begin to build your marketing around those concepts. To get the message out, you can always choose from among all of the old traditional marketing channels. But there are so many new modes of communication available that you will want to investigate using those new channels as well. For example, why not let customers themselves share their feelings about your company through blog entries or micro-blog entries? (You might want to revisit the chapter on social media (page 63), where specific examples of this concept are discussed.)

In the end, I still believe that your best marketing is simply to **execute.** Customers who have a fabulous experience with you will tell each other and then spread the word. But it never hurts to speed up the process of word-of-mouth through marketing. Listening to your existing customers and finding out just why they like you and what causes them return to you can be a tremendous source of marketing material.

PRACTICAL TACTICS: (Questions to ponder)
Are you using customer feedback in your marketing? Are you taking advantage of the depth of information captured from your current customers? How can you engage the voice of your existing customers to help "sell" your potential new customers?

Ensuring all units participate

"Is eating my vegetables optional?"

Helping franchisors and other multi-unit companies get stubborn operators to participate

Even if you've built a culture where a "complaint is a gift" and the senior executives understand that customer feedback is on the path to long-term financial success…still, the average company may have 10% to 15% of their operators (or franchisees) who "fight" against anyone measuring the customer experience in their units. This always reminds me of a certain 12-year-old who came home from school one day, with a look of disgust on her face, and said,

> **"Oh great, Dad; now they've made it so that you can go on the web at anytime and see my homework and test scores!"**

I haven't figured out a way to force someone to *want* to do something that will benefit them! Given the choice to participate, there will always be a few individual operators who just do not want to play. They will fight and whine and will blame everything there is to blame – "the survey isn't quite right," or "I already know everything my customers are thinking," or "my customers vote with their feet," or "customers make survey mistakes (<1%), so it's all invalid," or "this is costing too much in redemptions."

"It's broccoli, dear."
"I say it's spinach, and I say the hell with it."

It has been my experience that many unit-operators do not want the *added accountability* that comes with having their customer service results transparent to their management or their peers.

Did you see the movie where the main character is unable to lie and the exact truth always comes out of his mouth? Imagine if these same operators were in that situation and had to explain their real objections. Perhaps we'd hear something like: "I don't want anyone looking over my shoulder" or "my stores are performing badly and I don't want anyone to know," or "I don't exactly follow corporate policies," or "now I'll have to work harder to step up my performance." Given the hugely positive ROIs (returns on investment) that customer measurement has been proven to produce, why would any operator **_not_** want to know what their customers are thinking? This attitude baffles me every time I come across it.

Here are three approaches that successful companies have used effectively in this situation: (1) **_Sticks,_** (2) **_Carrots,_** and/or (3) **_Education._** Your company's culture will be the most important factor in determining which approach to take. Also, *your executive management's demonstrated commitment* will determine how committed your operators or franchisees will be. In short, if measuring customer feedback is "just another in a list of programs," then local operators will treat it as an elective, rather than as a required way of doing business.

The Stick Approach

Make customer satisfaction measurement a **_required part of doing business everyday._** Make it **_mandatory._** The most successful companies find a way to circumvent all the time and energy expended on this debate by simply ending the debate. They formally establish customer feedback as the #1 driver of operations improvement. It is not relegated to a "marketing research" project that is undertaken once a year, or to one or two mystery shops a month, but rather, customers are invited to provide feedback on *all* possible occasions, at *all* times. Customer experience measurement is *part of the company,* not just words.

If you make customer feedback measurement optional, then you are sending a very clear message that customer service is also optional!

Tactical Implementation Examples – STICK:
- Set *minimum* customer satisfaction levels as a condition of remaining a franchisee.
- *Publish lists* ranking units across areas, regions, or across the country, etc.
- Include customer satisfaction in the Franchise Disclosure Document *(FDD)* – (i.e., if you want to be a franchisee, you *will* participate).

- Make customer satisfaction scores an integral component of each local manager's *bonus*.
- Make sure customer satisfaction is one of the key metrics in the company's *balanced scorecard*.

The Carrot Approach

The "carrot" method relies on rewarding positive performers in order to: (1) recognize them for their success, and (2) motivate others to participate and to achieve.

Tactical Implementation Examples – CARROT:

- Reward the *units* with the highest *absolute* customer satisfaction score with extra incentives.
- Reward the *employees* with the highest *absolute* scores with extra pay, perks, promotions, and recognition.
- Reward the *units* and *employees* who have shown the greatest *improvement* over a previous time period.
- Recognize a *"rookie of the year"* (who may not have high scores yet, but is clearly gaining momentum).

The Education Approach

Over the years, I've noticed that large numbers of local operators and franchisees have not had exposure to some basic principles of business. For example, many view marketing programs as straight expenses regardless of the incremental sales a marketing program adds to their financial statements. Similarly, even though it has been proven time and time again that it costs significantly more to bring in a new customer than it costs to keep an existing customer; many franchisees find it difficult to spend even a small part of their local or national funds toward surveying and listening to their existing customers.

Tactical Implementation Examples – EDUCATION:

- Educate – *customer loyalty is the single biggest predictor of financial success.*
- Educate – it costs *5 to 10 times more to acquire a new customer* than to keep an existing one.
- Educate – one disgruntled customer can *use social media to tell millions* of people about their experience with you.

- Educate – locations that *commit* to measuring the customer experience and then *act* on that feedback, have been shown to make significant incremental profits over locations that don't. (The Harvard studies referenced on page 9 showed that companies can boost their profits 25% to 85% by retaining just 5% more customers.)

- Make sure to present revenues and costs of the program *together*. (If the incremental revenues and costs of the program remain buried in separate lines on an income statement and are never shown together in a return on investment (ROI) analysis, then those operators who believe they can "cost cut" their way to profitability will treat all customer feedback methods as a cost, rather than as a profit-generating investment.)

- Demonstrate *executive management's commitment* and *involvement* by having the CEO (or similar senior executive) send e-mails to five or six different unit managers each week with customer verbatim recordings attached (.mp3 files). In the CEO's e-mail, reference the positive or negative content of the customer's comment and praise the staff or ask about follow up. After just 3 or 4 weeks of this, the entire company will be very aware of senior management's involvement and will become motivated themselves to use the system.

Summary

One would be hard-pressed to find a corporate executive team that didn't advocate customer loyalty as an important part of their strategy. However, the implementation of the customer strategy requires continued commitment of resources and processes. Companies that present customer experience measurement as "optional" are sending a mixed message (i.e., "We want happy, loyal customers – but we just don't want to pay anything to get their feedback – nor do we want to mandate your participation"). This causes local operators and franchisees to doubt the commitment of the executive team and dilutes your credibility.

How to get your local operators and/or franchisees to participate in customer feedback systems?

1. Educate them about the return on investment (ROI) and the benefits of using customer feedback to drive operations improvement. Show them how they'll make more money over the long term.

2. Make it a part of your company's culture. Mandate participation. Listen to, but don't cave in to, the *"vocal minority"* who will whine

about the program. Post results. Hold people accountable. Put customer satisfaction results on an equal basis with financial and employee satisfaction results.

3. If you are unwilling or unable to mandate participation, then use the carrot approach: include customer satisfaction scores as a part of each manager's bonus calculation, openly reward those who excel in achieving the highest scores and those who show the most improvement. If you have an annual recognition dinner – make sure customer satisfaction and employee satisfaction results are included as award categories.

I have observed the greatest success where companies use a blended approach, summarized by the words: *educate*, *mandate*, and *reward*.

Regardless of which approach works best for you...

Make customer feedback and measurement a *"Brand Standard"* of your company.

PRACTICAL TACTICS: (Questions to ponder)

Does your company's culture thrive better under a <u>carrot approach</u>, or will you be better off (and save time and resources) <u>mandating</u> participation in measuring customer satisfaction? Can you blend these approaches to encourage participation? Have you spent enough time <u>educating</u> your unit operators on the ROI and incremental profits that come from putting the customer first?

Part VI

Customer Recovery and Follow-up

Recovering lost customers

"Sorry 'bout that…please come back!"

Accentuating service-lapse recovery

A lot of companies don't perform service-lapse recovery. They either haven't been taught about it, they don't believe it, or they have incorrectly assumed what one CEO said: "We have so much demand for our product that there will be two new customers walking through the door as one dissatisfied customer walks out." (How short-sighted can someone be?)

"This is what I call customer satisfaction!"

One definition of service-lapse recovery is those actions that a company takes to try and retain a customer before they lose them forever. Usually, the need for the recovery is because of a service error, an omission, or improper treatment. Of course, the best time to recover a customer is immediately after the mistake is made, before the customer leaves the site of the problem. But, if customers don't feel comfortable telling you about the problem face-to-face, then you may not get the feedback until later, after they have taken a feedback survey. Either way, recovering customers before they permanently defect has a big payoff. For example, research conducted by TARP found that customers who complained and were later satisfied are up to 8% more loyal than if they had never had a problem to begin with. And it costs significantly more to get a new customer than to keep the ones you've got.

You won't be able to use the customer satisfaction method advocated in the accompanying cartoon, but there are plenty of other ways to make them happy. An important first step is to make sure customers are valued correctly by employees.

Lifetime value of a customer

How do you value your customers? When they walk through the door are you thinking about the short-term sale, or do you value them for the lifetime of profits they could bring you? Let's say that you are in the pizza business. Your average ticket is something like $20.00 for a family. In walks a "ticked off" mom – what is she worth to you? $20.00? More? Let's check it out by doing the math:

Suppose she buys a pizza from you two out of every three weeks, for the next 30 years:

$$\$20.00 \text{ per visit } X \text{ 35 weeks } X \text{ 30 years} = \$21,000$$

The twenty-dollar customer is actually a $21 thousand-dollar customer! And actually she's worth much more if you count referrals she will make. But, here's the problem…we don't usually think that way. In fact, it is even more difficult to view a customer in that light when there may be a whole group of customers waiting in line behind her.

Here's a great story from the blog of Eric Sink (www.ericsink.com). He first tells us about his *"absurd"* service experience with a bank's credit card fee. He ends that part of the story by canceling his credit card. Then he tells us about Animal Outfitters and its owner, Mark:

> "Our new family pet is a white German Shepherd. We decided to feed Sophie a specialty food called Evo. The only store in our area which sells Evo is a very small place called Animal Outfitters. German Shepherds eat a remarkable amount of food. Monday I went in to Mark's store for another bag of Evo. He was sold out, but the next day, he brought in a bag of Evo from home, the one he had for his own dog. He measured out enough Evo to feed Sophie until the next week when his delivery was supposed to arrive. And despite my attempts to pay him, he didn't charge me a dime. I walked out of the store stunned. In the last week, two companies made *absurd* impressions on me.
>
> - I cannot imagine *ever* having another credit card with that bank.
> - I cannot imagine *ever* buying pet food anywhere but Animal Outfitters.
>
> When I first walked into Animal Outfitters, I wondered how this guy could possibly stay in business for so long. Now I know."

Bring them back!

Now that we know how much they're worth, we've got to focus on not losing a defecting customer due to something under our control. While the academic name is service-lapse recovery, it might just be easier to think of it as, "don't let $21,000 walk out your door!"

The grass is always greener in marketing, though

Here is another hidden secret: keeping customers you've already got is a whole lot more *boring* than getting new ones. With the new ones, you get to do fun stuff like marketing, and advertising, and promotions, and trade shows, and brochures, and press releases, and on and on. But keeping the ones you've got, that's just plain old "making them happy" – and it usually isn't very exhilarating stuff.

When I was at PepsiCo's Frito-Lay division in the 1980s we used a simple aphorism to explain the difference between new customer acquisition and existing customer retention.

"It is a whole lot easier to get Doritos eaters to buy more Doritos, than it is to get non-Doritos eaters to try Doritos."

Several research studies of the 80s and 90s looked at hundreds of customers across multiple industries and determined that it cost orders of magnitude more to acquire a new customer than to keep an existing one! Ask yourself this, *"How much money do we spend on keeping existing customers versus attracting new ones?"*

How to recover customers?

(Also, see the next chapter, "Cleaning up mistakes," for further discussion.)

Here is a generic set of recovery steps. Personalize it for your company. First, show your employees that you mean it by the way you allocate your *spending* and assign *bonuses*, then:

1. *Listen* to customer feedback.
2. Hold the local employee *accountable* to follow up.
3. *"Fix"* any internal problems, people, or processes.
4. *Immediately contact* the customer when appropriate.
5. Take *responsibility* for the error or the inconvenience.
6. *Give* them something of value (preferably something that will bring them back).
7. *Tell them* what you "fixed" (transparency).

How fast is "fast enough?"

Whenever I'm asked this question, I just throw it back in the inquirer's lap. I ask them, "When you have a bad service experience, how fast is *fast enough* for you?" This is one of those questions, where, if you have to ask it, you don't really "get" the concept.
The answer is Now! Rapido! Pronto! Inmediatamente! Git 'r done! The chart on the right illustrates a simple concept – the longer you wait, the less chance you have to recover that disappointed customer and bring them back to you for life. Do it. Do it now!

Give your employees the power to fix problems

To make service recovery real in your organization, you've got to give your employees the authority to fix customer issues where and when they happen. As customer service strategist, John Tschohl has said,

> "Empowerment is the backbone of service recovery. Employees must have the authority to do whatever it takes, on the spot, to take care of a customer to that customer's satisfaction—not to the satisfaction of the company. Most executives believe their employees are empowered. And most employees would agree—as long as they follow the policies and procedures set forth by the company. What that means is that there really is no empowerment."*

Remember, a big manual loaded with policies and procedures detailing exactly what a customer can get for being treated poorly isn't empowerment, it's simply following a manual.

PRACTICAL TACTICS: (Questions to ponder)

How much importance do you place on recovering defecting customers? Are your managers required to contact them (if they request follow-up)? Are your managers held accountable to follow-up? Do you train employees on the 'Lifetime Value' of a customer? How much can your employees spend to recover a customer without asking permission?

---

* (By John Tschohl, www.customer-service.com)

Cleaning up mistakes

"I apologize completely"

What to do when you make a mistake with a customer? *

THINGS TO DO

- Listen and let them explain. Don't interrupt.
- Thank them for the feedback and tell them *why* you appreciate it.
- Acknowledge and apologize, using the word "I," not "we."
- Explain (if you can).
- Make it right immediately for them (soft-cost compensation, upgrade, etc. – if appropriate).
- Commit to fixing the product, process, or person who caused it.
- Tell the customer exactly what you are going to do (or already did).
- Do what you committed to do.
- Follow-up to ensure satisfaction.

THINGS NOT TO DO

- Pretend there is no problem or blame the customer.
- Quote company rules and regulations.
- Tell them what you can't do. Do tell them what you <u>can</u> do.
- Leave the customer to deal with the issue alone.
- Try to win an argument.
- Embarrass the customer.
- Pass the buck within your company: "Bill didn't do his job…"
- Get emotional.

When they make a mistake, many people clam up and play ostrich – head in the sand – hoping that maybe those pesky customers will go away! In fact, it is the exact opposite approach that minimizes the damage of the mistake – acknowledge the problem openly and tell them what happened. The two most important steps are: **(1)** *explain* and *apologize,* and **(2)** *do it immediately!*

Here are some random things that I wish service providers would explain to me:

> This is *why* the plane just dropped 1,000 feet.
> This is *why* you were "on hold" for so long.
> This is *why* you can't check in to your room yet.
> This is *why* we are drawing this blood sample from you.
> This is *why* we can't serve you the fish tonight.
> *(Feel free to add your own personal issues to the list...)*

Paraphrasing Nietzsche...

"People can live with almost any *what* or *how,* if you give them a great *why*."

Apologize and move forward

One day as a boy, I was twirling a basketball in my family's front room in direct violation of my mother's parting instructions. The ball slipped, and I broke her favorite vase. When she came home, I decided to try a new tactic – quickly "come clean" and "take it like a man." So I did. "Mom, I broke the vase just like you said I would. I disobeyed you. I'm sorry." She accepted my apology. Nothing happened. No grounding. No guilt. Not even a lecture! I thought I'd discovered the Holy Grail or something. How can we apply that to business?

Nurse Next Door is a Vancouver home-health care company. Evidently, when they make a mistake they deliver a "Humble Pie" (apple) to their customer with a note that reads in part, *"We are humbled by our mistake and sincerely apologize for our poor service."* Wow! They get it. *Do you?*

"Mom, I broke the vase. *Here's why.* It won't happen again."

PRACTICAL TACTICS: (Questions to ponder)
What do your employees do when they make a mistake with a customer?

Helping difficult customers

"Blow out the dust"

Treating even difficult customers with respect

There are no dumb questions, but there are dumb people. So, what should you do when you have to present bad news to less sophisticated or very difficult customers?

There are several different approaches to consider. (One of them, "patient firmness," is best illustrated by the old story about the customer at the airport counter yelling loudly at the baggage department employee. Finally, the employee looks at the customer and says, "Sir, there are only two people on this entire planet who care about your bags, and one of us is losing interest!")

Perhaps the most important thing that one can do is to choose those employees with an innate sense of patience and long-suffering to deal with the most challenging customers. Further, we can train our employees to understand that **it doesn't do any good to prove to a customer that he's wrong.** The most practical method of helping problem customers involves listening carefully, then presenting information in a non-accusatory, non-blaming, diplomatic way.

Microsoft's Raymond Chen* tells the story of the customer who calls to complain that his keyboard isn't working. (Of course, it's unplugged.) However, if you try asking him if it's plugged in, "he will get insulted and say indignantly, 'Of course it is! Do you think I'm an idiot?' without actually checking."

Instead, Chen suggests saying something like, "Okay, sometimes the connection gets a little dusty and the connection gets weak. Could you unplug the connector, blow into it to get the dust out, then plug it back in?"

"They will then crawl under the desk, find that they forgot to plug it in (or plugged it into the wrong port), 'blow out the dust,' plug it in, and reply, 'Um, yeah, that fixed it, thanks.'"

Many requests for a customer to check something can be phrased this way.

(blogs.msdn.com/oldnewthing/archive/2004/03/03/83244.aspx)

Instead of telling them to check a setting, tell them to change the setting and then change it back "just to make sure that the settings are correct." Or take the example of the car renter who hasn't figured out that he needs to have his foot on the brake pedal before the ignition will start, you might say something like, "Would you please place your foot on the brake pedal, as a precaution while you start the engine?"

Sometimes we are our own worst enemy in these situations. We load up our products and services with jargon and acronyms that could dazzle even the brightest professor. It is always a good idea to have a non-interested third party review all materials to see if the materials can stand completely on their own, without additional explanation or translation.

It is also important to realize that some people are just not mechanically-minded or common-sense inclined. Customer service representatives need to be trained to be non-defensive, patient, empathetic, and especially innovative in coming up with creative ways of solving problems without offending the customer.

"Oh. You're obviously still angry. Please hold while I play another five minutes of soothing music to calm you down."

PRACTICAL TACTICS: (Questions to ponder)

How are difficult customers treated by your employees? Do you have scripting and training in place to help associates diplomatically answer customers' difficult or just plain old dumb questions?

Customer relations departments

"Let me speak to your supervisor!"

Customer relations departments – the buck stops here

How do you treat your customers who have taken the time to call into the customer relations department? One of the finest writings I ever read on customer service was *Championing the Customer,* * by Charles R. Weiser, the former head of British Airways customer relations department. Let me quote and paraphrase a few lines:

"This is the You-Must-Be-Wrong Department, formerly known as Customer Service."

"When I joined BA's customer relations department, I found an operation virtually untouched by the quality revolution that had caused the airline's reputation and fortunes to soar. In its *traditional defensive role*, customer relations had served as an investigator and adjudicator and had pursued four basic objectives:

1. **Insulate the company from unhappy customers.**
   (They conducted little analysis and didn't disseminate what they learned.)

2. **Assign blame for poor service rather than help the company learn how to prevent problems.**
   (The line functions saw the department as an adversary.)

3. **Buy dissatisfied customer's silence for the lowest possible price.**
   (Detailed rules for compensation had evolved over time. No flexibility.)

4. **Maximize the volume throughput by processing the largest possible number of complaints.**
   (Performance goals were focused on backlog, not on service to customers.)

* (See "Championing the Customer," C.R. Weiser, Harvard Business Review, Dec 1995.)

To champion the customer, the new management team instituted four *revised objectives*:

1. **Use customer feedback more effectively.**
   (Systems put in place and data distributed widely.)

2. **Prevent future service problems through teamwork.**
   (Frequent meetings held between line and staff.)

3. **Change pay-back compensation to meet customer's needs, not the company's.**
   (Dealt with each customer individually, with frequent reviews, rather than set policies and amounts.)

4. **Practice customer retention, not adjudication.**
   (Changed division measurements to customer-retention and ROI, rather than throughput and efficiency measures.)

I believe this description of "before" and "after" in British Airways' customer relations department is a *best-practice* approach that any company could follow in improving their customer relations department.

PRACTICAL TACTICS: (Questions to ponder)
Here's a suggestion: Read through the four descriptions of British Airways' customer relations department (the **before** list). Sound familiar? If it does, you've got your work cut out for you. But it is possible to turn around your company – BA was able to change an entire culture toward becoming customer champions.

Part VII

Tips and Tricks

Setting appropriate goals

Is 96% even an option?

Is there any worthy goal less than perfection?

During the great TQM craze of the 1990s, that I referred to earlier, I was speaking with one of the general managers of a large Marriott hotel. He was frustrated because his second-in-command had just posted a goal of 96% customer satisfaction for the hotel managers to achieve. Steve, the general manager, was not happy about aiming for anything less than 100%. He told his leadership team something I've never forgotten:

> ## "I want you all to stand at the front door today. As the customers arrive, please pin a red carnation on 4% of them, so we'll all know which customers to tick off today!"

Is there really any *goal* less than our best? Sure, we may want to *bonus* employees on a sliding scale to avoid penalizing them for a bad score from a customer who is a "perfectionist grader." You may even want to keep a set of internal versus external targets. (Because, in all fairness, there are sometimes structural barriers to reaching 100%.) We may not achieve it, but shouldn't our *goal* always be 100%?

For a goal, is there anything less than our best?

Do you remember when Xerox was *the* copier company? They had no strong competitors. But, over just a few years, they 'lost it.' And then, Xerox came back – stronger, more in tune. They attributed part of their resurgence to one of the most famous customer satisfaction studies ever conducted.* When they analyzed their customer feedback, they discovered a huge gap between those customers that answered '5' (the best score possible) and those that rated them lower. In fact, those who were "totally satisfied" were *six times* more likely to buy their products over the next 18 months, than those who rated them as "merely satisfied." Similar studies have now been done across many companies and industries, each showing a significant difference between customers who gave a rating of '5' vs. '4.'.

* *(See "Why Satisfied Customers Defect," T.O. Jones and E. W. Sasser, Jr. HBR, Nov. 1995.)*

Imagine watching a college football game on TV. One team has just scored a touchdown, and the TV cameras are sweeping the student section, full of enthusiastic, joyful students screaming, "We're number two! We're number two!" Never going to happen, right? Then how could we as business leaders be satisfied with anything less than aiming for the best? Here are two motivating pieces of advice to consider:

> **"Aim at perfection in everything, though in most things it is unattainable. However, they who aim at it, and persevere, will come much nearer to it than those whose laziness and despondency make them give it up as unattainable."**
>
> *(Lord Chesterfield)*

> **"It is better to aim at perfection and miss, than to aim at imperfection and hit it."**
>
> *(Thomas J. Watson)*

By ***aiming high*** we are not only keeping our sights high, we are also training our employees and our entire organization to always give their best and to deliver excellence.

PRACTICAL TACTICS: (Questions to ponder)

Regardless of where you choose to set your bonus measurements, where are you setting your company service goals? Do you act like an "excellence" company, or just a plodding-along, Eeyore-like place to work?

Measuring the total experience

Stop measuring only service <u>parts and pieces</u>. Measure the <u>entire experience</u>.

We don't think about it much, but it is very possible and quite common for each individual part of a customer's experience to be very good, but for the overall rating (and word-of-mouth referral) we receive to be poor. How can this be, you say? Let me share another experience from my early days in the hotel business.

Let's focus in on two fabulous service offerings delivered by full service hotels. One of the services is executed by the room service employees, and the other service is usually performed by the front office and night audit folks.

Service Offering #1
The concept of putting a guest's folio (invoice) under the door during the middle of the night revolutionized check-out. Instead of long lines and waiting for their folio in the morning at check-out, the folio is slid under the door at 4:00 am with all of the charges itemized, and a zero-balance printed, to give the customer peace of mind that there won't be any credit-card issues later. This is now common practice in the industry.

Service Offering #2
The other offering is on-time, in-room breakfast delivery with a time guarantee. So, if you request room service at 6:15am, then your breakfast will be there by 6:15!

Overall Experience:
So let's grade a theoretical hotel on its service:

1. I ordered breakfast at 7:00 am sharp. It was delivered at 6:59. **A+**

2. My zero-balance folio was placed under my door at 4:00 am. **A+**

3. *Overall experience* at the hotel? **C-**

But why? What went wrong? Each individual service offering was executed perfectly? So, what's the big problem?

Because the breakfast charge wasn't included on the folio! My credit card is going to be charged again, thus negating the benefit and convenience that the under-the-door folio service is supposed to create in the first place. (By the way, hotels have now satisfactorily fixed this issue in various ways: pre-billing breakfast, making a second credit card slip, etc.)

This type of experience (where the pieces are perfect, but the total isn't) is actually more common in service businesses than one might expect. It is important to guard against the trap of perfectly delivering individual parts and pieces of services, yet leaving a bad taste in the customer's mouth about the *overall* experience – the way the pieces do (or don't) fit together. Fixing such subtle weaknesses requires careful evaluation and effort. It requires viewing the *entire experience* through the customer's eyes.

Most problems need to be fixed twice: (1) once right away to alleviate the *symptom*, and (2) a later process change to fix the *root cause*. The immediate need is to fix the customer's problem. Then you need to dig deeper, and isolate the process error that is allowing the problem to occur. This is especially true when monitoring the service quality of the entire experience. If you just fix the visible symptoms you might miss the underlying root issues that are causing the complete experience to be poor.

PRACTICAL TACTICS: (Questions to ponder)

Have you diagrammed the entire customer experience of your firm? When was the last time you personally experienced the <u>entire process</u> that a customer experiences when he or she buys from you?

Managing the evidence

Perception is reality. What determines perception?

Epictetus, the Greek philosopher said:

"What concerns me is not the way things are, but rather the way people <u>think</u> things are."

This is truly one of the most interesting things I've studied over the years about customer service quality and execution. It's a little hidden secret that many companies never seem to understand. Here's what brand-guru David Aaker said:

"Achieving high quality is not enough; actual quality must be translated into <u>perceived</u> quality."*

Because we don't have the experience or the know-how to judge some things, we often resort to using substitutes to help us gauge quality. How do people quickly size-up the skills of a surgeon? Not knowing if he cheated his way through medical school, we are left to use the physical evidence that we have at our fingertips. So, many patients end up judging doctors by their bedside manner and by the neatness of their waiting room!

Let's say that an anxious customer sits down on an airplane and is sitting there wondering about the safety of the plane. When she pulls down the tray table in front of her, it is filthy – left over from a previous passenger.

At this point, it would not be uncommon for her to think to herself, "How can I trust this airline to maintain the complexities of keeping this huge airplane and its engines maintained and safe, *if they can't even keep a tray table clean?"*

Listen to this insightful comment, "The perception of a product is shaped to a large extent by the things that the consumer can comprehend with his five senses - tangible things. But a service itself cannot be tangible, so reliance must be placed on *peripheral* clues."**

---

* *(From "Managing Brand Equity," D. A. Aaker, The Free Press, 1991.)*

** *(From "Breaking Free From Product Marketing, " by G. L. Shostack, Journal of Marketing, April, 1977.)*

Here are some other common examples of clues that customers use to judge:

- **Home painting**   Appearance of the uniform.
- **Car repair**   Brand name and shop appearance.
- **Mail service**   Slogan: "Neither snow, nor rain, nor heat nor gloom of night"...can stop the US Postal Service.
- **Cars**   Solid door closure, cupholders.
- **Hotels**   Curb appeal, signage, website.
- **Retail**   Guarantees and hassle-free return policies.

In situations like these, companies must not only produce quality products and services, but also provide the customer with physical evidence or other kinds of clues to <u>help him make decisions about quality.</u>

This is called...

*"Managing the Evidence"**

Managing the evidence should include: **every type of communication** your company makes, from advertising to invoices, press releases to websites to call center language. Clues **reminding your customers of the differences** between "bad service," and the good service you are providing, so they will know what they are getting. Your **atmosphere and environment** - don't you hate it when the surrounding noise (or even the music) is so loud in a restaurant that you can't carry on a conversation? Don't forget smell. I had a client whose sandwich shop was located in a mall right next to a beauty salon and the smells of the chemicals used for "permanents" drove her customers away. **Interpersonal skills** of high-contact employees should be fine-tuned. My last doctor's appointment, the receptionist was doing her nails, didn't look up, and muttered "'kelp you?" **Employee appearance and attitude** - at Disney, employees are called "cast members" and they are always "in costume" and "on stage" – even the grounds crew. **Process flow -** the steps it takes to complete the transaction. **Flexibility. Price. Guarantees. Responsiveness and Urgency.** The examples are many, but the idea is critical.

PRACTICAL TACTICS: (Questions to ponder)

Are you in a business where customers are making decisions about your quality by using trivial substitutes to measure you? How are you scoring? Are you "Managing the Evidence" that your customers see?

* (From "Breaking Free From Product Marketing, " by G. L. Shostack, Journal of Marketing, April, 1977.)

Practical, tactical, useful

Things to do to make the magic flow

Practical ideas for making this all work

(With some adjustments in terminology and implementation, the following ideas will apply equally well to food and retail outlets, call centers, home service, banking, and most other service environments.)

Consider this chapter the blue-collar, working summary of tactics you can use to transform customer feedback into customer service improvements. Of course, there are far too many ideas to print here, so consider this a starter-list to get your creative juices flowing.

Here's a simple model for thinking about this issue. **Your main tactical levers to ensure motivation and delivery of great customer service** are:

- Alignment and communication
- Senior management commitment and involvement
- Recognition and appreciation
- Compensation and reward structures
- Engaging your employees
- A structured process for using customer feedback
- Coaching and training
- Setting specific goals for improvement or emulation

Alignment and communication

It is essential that you have the "buy-in" of your unit managers (or franchisees) and total alignment of their activities with the direction the company is taking. So, publish a clear set of company goals for customer satisfaction and loyalty, and then support alignment behind those goals by communicating, communicating, and over-communicating. Employees perform best when they know how their actions will affect both customer satisfaction and the company's success. So, tell them!

Tactical ideas

In best-practice companies, communication takes place using traditional means, such as newsletters, back-office bulletin boards, short "refresher" training tips, weekly staff meetings, posted results and posters, as well as through electronic news, e-mail, company media, central voice mail, and intranet. In addition, leading companies use cross-functional teams and role-plays as another way to ensure that all employees understand and act on the same information.

Senior management commitment and involvement

Let's face it, programs come and go. Corporate staff members sometimes create "flavor-of-the-month" projects that eventually burn out. Your employees will be watching to see if your executives are truly committed to customer experience measurement and to long-term customer loyalty. If there are doubters on the management team, the program will fall apart.

Tactical ideas

1. One of the biggest clues to the strength of senior management's commitment will be the way that customer experience feedback is presented and the words used to describe it. Is it a "program," or "the way we do business?" Are passive words like "might," "should," and "could" used to describe it and its benefits, or do you describe it using active words like "will deliver," "required participation," and "your commitment?"

2. Earlier, I presented one of my favorite practices for demonstrating that executives really believe in measuring customer service. It's a simple idea: each week, the CEO sends e-mails to 5 or 6 different unit managers with a customer recording about their location attached (small .mp3 files). In the e-mail, the CEO references the customer comment and if it is positive feedback, he praises the employee or process mentioned. If it's negative, he asks for clarification and follow-up. It won't take long for the entire company to know that the CEO is actually logging on to the customer feedback system and is committed to the process.

Recognition and appreciation

As an employee, is there a greater reward than a pat on the back? Scores of human resource studies have concluded that the number one motivator for employees is not money, but rather, recognition and appreciation. Employees want to know that their efforts are helping their company succeed. Positive reinforcement of individual employees and groups of employees is the most effective way to reinforce the service behaviors that you are trying to establish.

Tactical ideas

Here are some of my *favorite recognition ideas:*

1a. At the annual awards gathering (banquet, meeting, ceremony) present awards for all, or even just a portion of the following *customer satisfaction* categories:

	Region/ Franchisee	Store	Employee
Highest Absolute Score – CSI	XYZ: 97%	SLC: 98%	Judy: 99%
Greatest % Improvement – CSI	ABC: +16% pts.	LAX: +11% pts.	Bill: +22% pts.
Rookie of the Year – CSI	PQR: 83%	MID: 84%	Bob: 97%

If you are able to present more awards, then in addition to "customer satisfaction index" (CSI), or "overall satisfaction," you might want to present awards for "highest survey volume," or "highest survey volume per transaction," "highest scores for an Area or DMA," "highest scores on specific variables," etc.

[NOTE: It is important to present awards for both high absolute scores and biggest score improvement. Also, the "Rookie of the Year" award is an idea I have found great success using over the years. It motivates not only the recipients, but also all the new employees who will join the company over the coming year.]

1b. Present similar awards for successful results in *employee satisfaction* categories.

2. On an ongoing basis at each location, *post the results* of customer surveys for all to see. Metrics presented might include: survey volume, customer satisfaction scores, product scores, specific service scores *(friendliness, speed, knowledge, cleanliness, etc.)*, rankings of teams or employees, trend charts, customer call-back percentages *(or how many were called back within X hours)*, employees with the most positive comments, stores/teams or employees with the fewest alerts, employee who helps her peers the most, employees or teams that surpass targeted goals and standards, etc.

Every company has their own style and culture. You choose what is best for yours. Personally, I prefer to use positive reinforcement *(lowest alerts, highest positive customer comments)* rather than focus on the negatives.

Compensation and reward structures

Cash still matters. Adding customer satisfaction metrics to compensation and/or performance bonuses helps solidify an employee's commitment to your company and your customers. Companies that truly understand the economics of their business recognize the incredible costs "hidden" in employee turnover, which then translates to poor customer service. So, *focus on employee retention to improve customer retention* and loyalty.

Remember the opening statement of this book? Here it is:

"The major drivers of a company's financial success can be traced back to truly loyal customers who return and recommend your business over and over, and loyal employees who, by their longevity and experience, become increasingly more productive, thereby providing better service and contributing even more to the company's bottom line."

Good, happy, tenured employees who are compensated and recognized for their contributions are the key to good, happy, loyal, and profitable customers!

Tactical ideas

1. Use a balanced scorecard (see chapter titled "The balanced scorecard," page 125). Make ESI (Employee Satisfaction Index) and CSI (Customer Satisfaction Index) a part of every manager's bonus. Many companies compensate <u>each</u> associate at year-end with a performance bonus based on their quality and personal contribution. However, while individual recognition is important, sometimes team recognition works better. Consider also compensating at the team level.

2. In addition to formal bonus programs, I strongly suggest incorporating weekly, monthly, or quarterly rewards and recognition. Incentive programs should be based on survey volumes as well as on customer satisfaction results. Here's a laundry list of incentives to stimulate your thinking: cash, prizes, temporary increase in hourly wage, store discounts, trips, company product discounts, go home early on a Friday, special business cards or name tags, certificates and plaques, $5 to every employee with more than eight surveys, prepaid phone cards, movie tickets, video rentals, choice of shifts, employee of the month, boss for a day, etc.

3. As mentioned earlier, by far the best reward for me as an employee is recognition of my efforts, including special public recognition by my boss in front of my peers. So celebrate the wins! "Catch your employees" doing something right, or going the extra mile! (Remember the old adage, *"Praise in public, counsel in private."*) Let your other associates or units join in the celebration of great performance. Acknowledge outstanding performance quickly. Strive to create an almost competitive feeling of, *"If he or she can do it, so can I."*

Having briefly mentioned it, let me comment specifically on counseling poor performers. Once you have collected feedback about an employee from multiple customers, trust your customers' perception. Use it (as presented in your customer feedback system) to determine which associates are not achieving company standards and agreed-upon goals.

Personally counsel under-performers. Set specific goals for improvement – with due dates. Document conversations and clearly outline expectations. Determine appropriate next steps for those associates or managers who are not able to bring their performance up to standard. Do not let problem areas linger. If a change is necessary, do it now. It will be better for all parties involved.

Engaging your employees

One of the most overlooked areas of motivating employees to improve their performance is to fully involve them in the success of the company. This means continually asking for their input. It also means giving them the opportunity to make independent customer service decisions.

Tactical ideas

Here are a couple of examples:

1. I love flying Southwest Airlines for lots of reasons, but my favorite reason is the freedom that their employees are given to express themselves over the microphone. Perhaps you've heard some of the more famous stories attributed to them:

   • As the plane landed and was coming to a stop, a lone voice came over the loudspeaker: *"Whoa, big fella. WHOA!"*

- "In the event of a sudden loss of cabin pressure, oxygen masks will descend from the ceiling. *Stop screaming*, grab the mask, and pull it over your face."

- After taking off, the pilot got on the speaker and said, "Bear with me folks, *this is my first time*."

Southwest allows its employees the independence to use humor creatively with their customers. This makes Southwest feel to me like the employees care more about their company. What similar actions could you take?

2. Involving your employees also means letting them know how their actions affect company results: "When you do X well, then the company achieves Y, and that will generate Z rewards for you."

3. Another great idea for engagement is to have top-performing employees lead staff meetings and training sessions to teach others what they do that generates their success.

A structured process for using customer feedback

One of the most practical things you can do to incorporate customer feedback into your business is to establish a standard schedule for managers at all levels to review the feedback and then take action.

Tactical ideas

By establishing expectations of involvement right up front, you are letting the entire company know that they will be held accountable for understanding the system of customer feedback and using it to improve their operations.

The following table shows just one example of what a standard feedback review schedule might look like.

ESTABLISH A STANDARD SCHEDULE TO REVIEW FEEDBACK
(Sample Suggested Schedule)

Who? \ When?	Monthly	Weekly	Daily
Executive Management	Review SUMMARY results of units Review at least 5+ voice/text messages Set goals for improvement with middle managers	As needed	As needed
Middle Management	Review DETAILED results of units Set goals with unit managers	Review alerts Review at least 10+ voice/text messages	As needed
Unit Management	Review SPECIFIC results with associates Set goals with associates *Note: If customer feedback is collected at the associate level, the goal-setting sessions will be more impactful.*	Review weekly reports with associates and set goals Review every customer voice/text message Present voice/text messages during training	Review Alerts Call to recover unhappy customers and to reinforce very happy customers

- Each level of management should have a standard schedule of reviewing customer feedback.
- The closer to the customer, the more detailed the review should be.
- Executive management should routinely "get dirty in the details" to hear what the customer is saying.

Coaching and training

*"If you always do what you've always done, you will always get what you've always gotten."** Best-practice companies put heavy emphasis on providing extensive and frequent training for their front-line employees. Typically, new employees receive lots of formal training up-front, with ongoing training offered to long-term employees and management. This training is provided using a variety of methods and includes a wide range of courses. These companies recognize that training:

- Gives the employee more skills.
- Improves their self-esteem.
- Deepens their committment.
- Increases the value of the entire company.

There is another kind of important training, however, and that is ad hoc, nip-a-problem-in-the-bud training that should occur as soon as the need becomes apparent.

Tactical ideas

Suggested steps for coaching and training (either formal or ad hoc):**

1. **Review the issue**
   Explain the desired outcome. Before you teach the "*what*," explain the "*why*." Also, point out the difference between "activity" and "achieving results."

2. **Explain the correct process**
   Review the activity verbally from beginning to end.

3. **Demonstrate**
   Clearly demonstrate the activity, inviting questions.

4. **Have the student explain and demonstrate**
   Step-by-step, have the trainees teach you back the skill.

5. **Set expectations for follow-up and review**
   Set a timeline for follow-up.

---

* (Anonymous. Popularized by Anthony Robbins.)

** (Some training programs use a variation: EDIP. (Explain, demonstrate, imitate, practice.)

Practical, Tactical, Useful!

Additional:

>   a. **Provide employees/teams with appropriate tools**
>   Provide the right tools, aids, computers, and equipment that will help employees be more effective.
>
>   b. **Encourage, inspire, and motivate**
>   Act like a leader. Rally the troops. Provide them emotional uplift.

Setting specific goals for improvement or emulation

Niccolo Machiavelli once said, **"Make no small plans for they have no power to stir the soul."** A crucial key to continuous improvement is choosing a goal and sticking to it.

Let me quote from one of my clients:

> *"I've been taking the reports each week and reviewing them with the associates, one-on-one. Then, I invite them to set their own goals. The improvement has been remarkable."*

Tactical ideas

Set specific goals for improvement or emulation. (One example process is outlined on the next page). Review the goals with the employee or unit manager.

>   Example goals…
>
>   1. **Top performer:**
>   - "I will improve my score from 94 to 96 next month."
>   - "Within 30 days, I will document what I've done to achieve my high scores, so the rest of the operation can learn from my experience."
>
>   2. **Lowest performer as ranked against peers:**
>   - "My team will move from the bottom of the rankings to the middle of the rankings within two months."
>   - "I will improve customer perception in this area from 48% to 55% by next month."

3. **Lowest performer as measured against company standards:**
   - "I will move my performance into the acceptable range within 60 days."
   - "I will increase my service score from 74 to 78 next week."

4. **Those whose performance is trending downward:**
   - "I will stop the decline in "speed of service" by next week."
   - "By the end of next month, my team will get back to where we were 3 months ago."

Some other goals to consider:
- "I will increase the number of surveys for my store from 42 per month to 77 per month."
- "My team will suggest add-on products to at least 75% of our customers next month."
- "By the end of next week, my customers will perceive that they were greeted 85% of the time."

Setting Goals *(adapted from Peter Drucker)*	
Specific:	A specific goal has a much greater chance of being accomplished than a general goal. Ask who, what, where, when, why?
Measurable:	To determine if your goal is measurable, ask questions such as...How much? How many? How will I know when it is accomplished?
Attainable or **A**chievable:	Begin seeing previously overlooked opportunities to bring yourself closer to the achievement of your goals.
Realistic or **R**easonable:	A goal is realistic if you truly believe that it can be accomplished and you are willing and able to try.
Tangible or **T**imely:	A goal is tangible when you can experience it with one of the senses, and timely when it has a finish date.

Once you've helped an associate or manager set their goals, make sure that they are written down. As the old saying goes:

"A goal not written is only a wish!"

So, set goals. Make them a stretch, but achievable. Follow a process and write them down. And then, hold yourself and your employees accountable for progress toward achieving those goals.

Elbert Hubbard summed it up this way:

"Many people fail in life, not for lack of ability or brains or even courage, but simply because they have never organized their energies around a goal."

"I understand what you're trying to do here, Tom, but I'd appreciate it more if you'd actually do it."

PRACTICAL TACTICS: (Questions to ponder)

Have you thought through the main levers listed at the beginning of this chapter? How does your company stack up? What tactics have you gleaned from this starter list? What other ideas can you come up with? List at least four things you are going to start doing immediately. Have you asked your employees for their input into what would motivate them? Are you sending a clear and consistent message of the importance of customer service and customer experience measurement? Do you, yourself have goals aimed at making this effort successful?

Measuring the ROI (return on investment)

Does customer feedback work?

Two questions on this subject often get co-mingled.
(1) Does <u>delivering</u> exceptional customer service improve revenues and profits?
(2) Does a rigorous and consistent commitment to <u>measuring</u> customer feedback increase revenues and profits?

For an overview on the answer to question one, I direct you back to the chapter entitled "Results: why do this?" (page 9). In that chapter (and throughout the book), I provide references to multiple research studies that have proven the significant economic impact of treating customer service as an organization's highest priority.

In this chapter, I provide some tactical methods that can help isolate and quantify the economic impact of <u>measuring</u> customer feedback. While it isn't always possible to separate the benefits of customer feedback from all of the other service components, the basic premise is straightforward – do those stores, teams, or individual employees who gather and act upon customer feedback perform better and deliver more value to the company? Do an organization's profits increase over time because it listens to its customers, and improves its operations based on what the customers say?

The results of our clients' experience on this subject have been very compelling:
(1) Collecting customer feedback and using that feedback to improve operations has been a **key driver** in increasing customer satisfaction scores (e.g. **CSI**), and,
(2) There is a **direct correlation** between **high CSI** scores and **incremental sales.**

Often, the results are so obvious that rigorous statistical analysis can be supplemented with simple **visual correlation,** such as the one at right, which shows the strong correlation between a high CSI (customer satisfaction index) and the resultant increase in sales growth two months later.

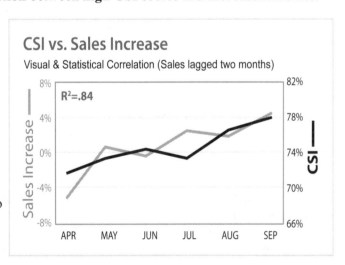

CSI vs. Sales Increase

Visual & Statistical Correlation (Sales lagged two months)

$R^2=.84$

There are many ways to statistically measure the results of gathering and acting upon customer feedback – each with varying levels of sophistication, complexity, and precision. The most important part of measuring is not just the Payback or ROI modeling, but rather the <u>incrementality</u> attributable to service and feedback measurement. I've chosen to present simplified examples of three methods that can be used to ascribe hard results to measuring customer feedback:

(1) Compare the results of **participating** versus **non-participating units** (control group) over time.
(2) If you have no control group, divide all participating units into groups based on how each performed on some proxy of "commitment to using feedback." (In essence, try to divide participating units into buckets of **high, medium, and low users** of customer measurement.) Compare the groups over time.
(3) Determine the "lifetime value" of a customer and then extrapolate **the total value saved by retaining customers** who were "recovered" before they could permanently defect.

Example 1:

(With a control group)

In this example, we compare participating units against a control group. First we "normalize" the difference in annual sales before the pilot (not shown here). Then we calculate incremental sales by comparing the sales results of the participating vs. non-participating units both before and after the customer feedback pilot time period (chart 1). Next, we subtract from incremental sales the cost of measurement and the average cost of incentive redemptions (including breakage), and then subtract the <u>variable</u> cost of incremental products/services sold (and incremental labor, if any) – to arrive at net incremental profit.

Chart 1

Chart 2

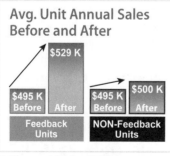

Avg. Unit Annual Sales Before and After

$529 K

$495 K
Before / After

$495 K
Before / $500 K After

Feedback Units

NON-Feedback Units

Net Incremental Sales +5.86%
(Feedback users vs. control group)

Simple Return on Investment Calculation
Participating vs. Control Units

Incremental Sales	+ 5.86%	$29,000
Cost to measure	- 0.25	($ 1,248)
Avg. incremental redemption	- 0.14	($ 690)
Net Incremental Sales	5.47%	$27,062
Avg. incremental variable cost	28.00%	($ 8,120)
Net Incremental Profit		$18,942

Differences due to rounding.

Sometimes it is not possible to measure against a control group, because 100% of all locations participate in measuring customer feedback from the start.

Measuring the ROI

Example 2:

(Comparing "heavy" feedback users vs. "light" feedback users)

In this example we use surveys/thousand customers as a <u>proxy</u> for a store's "commitment to feedback." Chart 3 shows the strong correlation between surveys/thousand and how frequently employees recommend an upsell product. Chart 4 then shows that the more frequently a product is recommended, the greater the sales result. In summary, surveying leads to behavior which leads to results.

Chart 3

Chart 4

In this example, those units who collect more surveys per capita (and ostensibly are more committed to feedback and more active in using it) have employees who ask upsell questions more consistently and therefore they sell more product consistently. Economic results of high, medium, and low users can then be compared using a Payback model or an ROI calculation like the one shown in chart 2.

This method is not as precise as measuring vs. a control group, but in a situation where all units are participating, the next best approach is to compare those who are gathering and using the feedback against those managers who don't demonstrate as strong a commitment. In the example above, we used surveys/thousand customers as a proxy for commitment - other proxies for commitment might include usage statistics such as - frequency of logging-in to the feedback system, % of problem alerts followed up on, etc.

Example 3:

(Extrapolate the lifetime value of "saving" customers before they defect)

In this example (see chart 5), we first calculate the "lifetime value" of a customer - how much a customer pays us over their lifetime, rather than on just one visit. This helps us truly quantify how much we put at risk each time a customer defects due to poor service.

Then, in chart 6, we conservatively estimate how much lifetime revenue we risk each month by observing how many customers request call backs due to poor service and conservatively estimating (in this example) that 1 out of 20 of them are at risk of defection. The analysis demonstrates a strong economic case for measuring customer service, and recovering "at risk" customers, even if the already conservative assumptions are cut in half over and over again.

Chart 5

Lifetime Value of a Customer

Average Ticket Size	$ 29.00
Average visits per year	18
Avg. # of customer years	22
Lifetime Value of a Customer	**$11,484**

Chart 6

Lifetime Revenues at Risk Each Month

Surveys/month 100 X 850 locations	85,000
% alerts (customers requesting call backs)	3.3 %
Customers requesting callbacks	2,805
% of alerts at risk (conservative est.)	5.0 %
Customers potentially at risk	140 /mo
Lifetime revenues at risk each month	**$1.6 million**

($11,484* 140 at risk customers/month)

Note:

Additional analysis (not shown here) may include isolating the economic benefit of bounce-back revenues from the survey incentive, increased referrals from loyal guests, reduced costs to service loyal customers, reduction in customer churn, the value of customer information collected, increased employee engagement and productivity, increased loyalty from recovered customers, and the long-term impacts of improved service delivery on your brand.

Summary

There is a demonstrated **link** between delivering and measuring customer service and achieving positive business results. The overriding consensus of academic theory and real-life examples is that there is a direct link between creating loyal customers and employees, collecting their feedback on service experiences, and achieving superior profits. The research supports common sense. Measurement reinforces positive behaviors and alerts you to negative behaviors. This guides you to make operational improvements, which drive satisfaction, which is required for loyalty to grow.

The conclusion?

Service **measurement**, followed by **action**, drives **revenues and profits**!

PRACTICAL TACTICS: (Questions to ponder)

Have you measured the economic benefit of gathering and responding to customer feedback? Do your employees understand the concept of the "lifetime value" of a guest? Have you demonstrated through analysis the linkage at your organization between high customer satisfaction and increased sales?

Elusive results?

Why aren't the lines trending upward?

We're doing the work, where are the results?

In dealing with hundreds of companies over the years, I have documented clear and direct correlations between measuring customer service, increased customer satisfaction scores, and increased financial results. Results of research with clients have paralleled results of major cross-industry academic studies on hundreds of companies. (Please see the previous chapter, and the "References and Recommend Reading" index.)

To sum it all up – it works!!

Having said that, there have been a *few exceptions* where results did not seem, on the surface, to be favorable. Let me introduce these exceptions by sharing two rare, but important, questions I have been asked:

1. **"I'm collecting customer feedback; why haven't my customer satisfaction scores budged?"**

2. **"My service scores are rising; why aren't my sales and profits also rising?"**

Because several of the potential answers to these questions overlap, I'll address both of them together.

WRONG ANSWER

Let me point out that the ***absolute wrong response*** to either of these situations is to discontinue or cut back on collecting customer feedback. In fact, collecting customer feedback may be the ***only way*** that you can find out what you should do to get out of a downward sales spiral! (When a business in trouble wants to drop customer surveys, I am reminded of a joke where the man says to his wife, "I just read that drinking beer is bad for your health, so I'm going to stop!" She responds with disbelief, "*You're* going to stop *drinking*?" He replies, "No, I gotta stop *reading*.") Likewise, discontinuing customer surveys because your business is struggling, is blaming the wrong thing. **TIP:** *Never stop listening to your customers!*

Accountability and action

Earlier in the book (page 113), I discussed the single most prevalent cause for failure to see results – that is a lack of action, commitment, and follow-up by the company. Because I think it is so vitally important, I'm going to repeat a paragraph from the earlier chapter. Generally, when a company is not seeing improved results, either financially and/or in service scores, I have observed the following:

> "The company has been conscientious in its effort to measure satisfaction. They have been completely committed to obtaining and communicating results. But, they have had no commitment to improving the level of service; no follow up on needed training, no inclusion of customer satisfaction results in bonus plans, and no one has been held accountable for following up with and recovering customers who complained about a service lapse."

A lack of accountability for action is the *single biggest factor* in those companies that are measuring the customer experience but not seeing improvements in their base metrics.

"Another month of terrible results.
Oh, when will it end?"

However, once in a while, I see a company that *is* taking action on their customer feedback and still not seeing desired results. What other potential explanations are there for a company's neutral or negative outcome? Uncovering the true cause may require some concerted analytical "digging" on your part. I suggest the following list as a good place to begin your exploration.

Macroeconomic issues

In a recession, you may possibly have customers who are ecstatic with your service, but just not enough of them. If you are consistently listening to your customers, your competitors are probably worse off than you are. Don't give up that advantage. **TIP: *Don't lose focus on customer satisfaction, especially in a recession.***

Unique business issues (specific to your company)

- **Example: takeover rumors**

  A few years back, I watched while the customer satisfaction scores of a fast-casual restaurant chain remained flat, as sales were dropping. At that time, the company was a takeover candidate by a restaurant chain of lesser reputation. In response to the rumors, their most discriminating customers began to defect, leaving behind a diminished customer base, and a higher proportion of "easy-to-please" customers, which kept the customer satisfaction scores from plummeting, even as sales were falling.

- **Example: location, location, location**

  Let's say you're a hotel manager and a competitor opens a new hotel down the street, closer to the freeway. Your service may be impeccable, but your product just became inferior. You have happy customers, just fewer of them.

  TIP: *Understand how your company's unique business issues (and especially rumors of business issues) are affecting your employees and your customers.*

Sampling instead of canvassing the population

I once had a call center client who wanted to reduce costs, so they only surveyed a small subset of customers who had spoken with their phone representatives. The company couldn't understand why one of their peer competitors generated so much success using post-call surveys, while they remained stagnant. Try as I might, I couldn't convince them that the few extra dollars they would spend evaluating *all* of their call center agents would be significantly offset by having more reliable customer feedback, reduced employee turnover costs, and having happier, more loyal customers. **TIP:** *Do not sample. Take a continuous movie, not a snapshot.*

Fashions and trends

I've learned to never underestimate the power of customer emotions and the "herd mentality" – particularly those emotions relating to trends among youthful consumers. Let's say that you are a clothing store chain, aiming at the teenage and early 20's target market. Then, fashion trends suddenly turn away from you. Those customers that continue to buy your products love your clothing and love your service, and rate you that way on customer feedback surveys. The "masses," however, are no longer frequenting your stores and are flocking to your competitors. Customer satisfaction remains steady, but sales decline. **TIP:** *Make sure that your customer service efforts are not being damaged by underlying trends.*

Price/value and economic issues

This next example is a bit facetious, but helps me communicate the issue clearly. Imagine being able to purchase your favorite luxury car for under $10,000. As a result, the car company sells hundreds of thousands of cars, the customers are overjoyed with happiness and service, yet the company goes bankrupt. **TIP:** *Poor underlying economics cannot be salvaged, even by fantastic customer service.*

Diminishing returns on the last dollar spent

Is it possible to "over-serve" your customers? No. However, is it possible to over-serve your customers to the point of *economic disaster*? You bet it is. Economists have a principle they call, "the law of diminishing returns." This law applies directly to the structural resources expended on going after "that last 3%" of customer satisfaction. An insightful example of this issue is the decision that each call center manager has to make regarding "abandoned calls" (calls where the customer hangs up before speaking with an agent). In theory, the goal for abandoned calls should be 0%. But this is <u>structurally</u> not possible, due to the daily cyclical swings in call volume at most call centers. So, most call centers target an "acceptable level" of call abandonment, say 4%. By far, the most sensitive variable affecting abandoned call rates is employee staffing. Because calls arrive at most call centers in peaks and valleys during a day, the call center manager is tasked with trying to staff as efficiently as possible for the peaks, without having a lot of agents twiddling their thumbs one hour later when call volume tapers off. The manager therefore has to make a cost-service trade-off. I've heard many a rookie manager say something like, "Under my watch, our abandoned call rate will fall to less than 1%." In order to accomplish this level, her labor costs immediately skyrocket, and eventually she has to reverse her

"The voicemail roulette wheel has landed on 'call abandoned'. If you would like to spin the wheel again, press 1."

position and tolerate some "acceptable level" of abandoned calls, or lose her job. **TIP:** *In some specific circumstances, trying to capture "that last 3%" of customer satisfaction may cost you more than it's worth.*

Incredibly high scores

Over the years, I've seen a few "category killer" clients whose customer feedback scores on products and/or services have been astronomically high. One company's stores averaged 95% on their customer satisfaction index. Is there no work to be done in such a situation? Is there "nowhere to go, but down?" Of course not. There is always room for improvement! We implemented a more aggressive scoring system that spread the distribution of the stores out a bit, and began focusing on more subtle improvements to their customer service, without losing the important focus on the basics. **TIP:** *For those of you who hover near perfection, there are always ways to further distinguish the "very best" from the "merely excellent." And, there are always services that can be improved in some way.*

"Home cooking" by employees who hand out survey invitations

The best ways to invite a customer to take a survey are those that cannot be directly affected by the employees in any way. (In retail and restaurants this would include printing the survey invitation on the receipt. In call centers, the company's automated voice system would present the invitation to each guest, or a guest-requested call-back would initiate the survey. In home service situations, the survey invitation might be printed on the work order or customer invoice.) With these methods, *all customers are given an equal opportunity to take a survey.* On the other hand, if employees are allowed to "pick and choose" who gets to take a survey, and there is no secondary check on them, invariably, some employees will try to manipulate their scores. This is usually attempted by withholding survey invitations from customers who have had a bad experience. **TIP:** *Choose a survey invitation method that is not subject to manipulation, that is routine, and automated.*

Time-lags between service delivery and results

Most repetitive customer service situations involve a purchase-and-repeat cycle that presents a time lag between the delivery of the service, and when company financial metrics are affected. For example, let's take the case of a man who gets his haircut every six weeks. On one occasion he has a miserable service experience. Let's say that this particular customer is forgiving and decides to give the hair salon another chance. When he returns, he once again has a bad experience. Now he's never coming back.

But the salon won't "miss" his revenues for another six weeks until he doesn't show up at his regular time. The total "elapsed time" between his first bad experience and the resulting dent in sales could be approximately 12 weeks. (It is possible that the revenue decline might kick in even sooner, if he starts telling all his friends "never go to this salon" after his second bad experience.) **TIP:** *The repeat purchase cycle of a business must be taken into account when trying to correlate changes in customer satisfaction levels to changes in financial results.*

Noise

"Noise" is the research professional's term calling out "all other" possible events, occurrences, or variables that might be influencing a lack of movement in business results. For example, let's say that a subset of a restaurant chain's stores runs a special discount promotion, or that a retail store runs an internal employee incentive, or a call center that needs to reduce expenses pays agents an extra bonus for shortening talk times. Each of these would impact results. Because business needs and programs are constantly changing, it is difficult to demonstrate correlated results unless you hold as many business variables as steady as possible for an evaluation period of time. **TIP:** *"Noise" may make actual correlated results difficult to isolate.*

SUMMARY

If your company is struggling with stagnant metrics (financial, customer satisfaction, or otherwise), do not be "penny-wise and pound foolish" by even thinking of discontinuing your customer feedback process. Don't "throw the baby out with the bath water." Rather, listen to your customers even more closely and look for causal factors that may be contributing to your stagnation. The first place to evaluate yourself is your company's commitment to local-manager accountability and action. If you believe you are truly giving it your best shot in this area, then dig deeper into one of the several potential explanations I have listed above, to see if one most closely fits your circumstance. A lack of immediately discernible results does not mean that customer involvement isn't working, it is. But unless you turn that customer feedback into action, you're just "collecting data," rather than embracing concrete steps toward improvement. Additionally, there are often extenuating circumstances and other variables present which are clouding the view of your forward progress. These need to be identified and removed from the data to be able to view a clear picture of results.

Front line employee impact

I am the face of our company!

Do your front-line employees know their importance to your organization?

(Do <u>you</u> truly understand their importance to your company?)

I often stop by the desk of our customer service reps, Ellie and Jordan, to remind them, "To 95% of the people who contact us, *you are Mindshare!"* Since the large majority of the administrative and support parts of our business are conducted over the phone, Ellie and Jordan are usually the first contact for most of the people who call our company. You have your own Ellies and Jordans in *your company* – they may be receptionists, CSRs, front-line servers, call center agents, etc. Their attitude impacts your reputation. Their bad day is your company's bad day. Their cheerfulness, empathy, and energy are bigger than any company sign you have on your building.

So, a couple of questions for you:

1. Do these good folks know their importance to the organization?
2. Do you have the right people in these jobs, and do you make them a priority?
3. Do they feel loved and appreciated?
4. Are they receiving customer feedback about their performance?

All of your good intentions can be erased by a single negative interaction with someone on your front lines.

> **Their bad day is your company's bad day.**

Several hospital studies over the years have listed the factors that were most correlated with the likelihood of a patient to recommend a hospital. Most of the top 10 factors were related to nurse and hospital staff and *only one or two of the variables even related to doctors!* This demonstrates why it is so vitally important to measure customer experiences all the way down to the employee (or the shift) level. Then, when the data has been compiled into actionable information and reports, it should be accessible to those on the front lines. ***The value of customer feedback information increases exponentially with its timeliness and usability by front-line workers.***

The goal of customer feedback measurement is not only to rank and list retail stores, or call center teams, or hospitals at the end of a month; it is to *immediately* understand employee-customer interactions at *every touch point!* Aggregate data is valuable, but in most cases it is the detailed data that leads to action at the unit level. It is the front-line employees who make or break your reputation.

"How may I neglect your call?"

"I'm in charge of insulting our customer's intelligence, you itty-bitty little man."

I really like this important reminder to the front-line worker * …

To Front-Line Employees

To the customer, you are the company. How good a job you do with them and for them will determine how successful your company will be. In your hands is the power to keep customers coming back.

You are the company.

---

* (From "Delivering Knock Your Socks Off Service," revised edition, by Kristin Anderson, and Ron Zemke, Amacom, January, 1998)

Aside from hiring the right people to begin with, and training correctly, what can your company do to ensure that front-line employees are delivering exceptional service? **Several studies have supported the common-sense notion that the way that front-line employees treat your customers will be strongly influenced by the way they are treated.**

Question: So, how should you treat your front-line associates?

Answer: This question is best answered by a sign on the kids' clubhouse door:

> ## "In this clubhouse, nobody act big, nobody act small, everybody act medium."*

I think the companies that do this right have removed a lot of the airs and egos and pomposities (yes, that is a word) that we all detest being around. (Hey, if there's an earthquake, we're all under the table together, right?)

I have a good friend who was the COO of a very large Midwest conglomerate and was being heavily recruited to become the CEO of a multi-billion dollar company on the East coast. This required a lot of travel back and forth at unusual times, while the company narrowed the field of candidates. Finally, the headhunters and the company couldn't decide between two equally-qualified finalists. To break the tie, they interviewed the pilots, chauffeurs, secretaries, and receptionists. My friend was easily chosen, because, as these front-line employees said in their own words, "He treated us like human beings, while the other gentleman paid us no attention."

These are your front-line employees. They **are** *your company* to most of your customers! How are you treating them?

PRACTICAL TACTICS: (Questions to ponder)
How do you treat your front-line associates? Are they aware of their importance as the face and voice of the company? Are they receiving appropriate priority in training, recognition, etc?

---

* *(From "Great Church Fights," L. B. Flynn, Victor Books, 1976.)*

Making hard decisions

Some important "pig" rules

So, why the title about pig rules? Because I've always loved a couple of little anonymous quotes about pigs:

1. **"Never put lipstick on a pig."***
2. **"Never try to teach a pig to sing – it wastes your time, and annoys the pig."***

In other words...

- **Don't try to dress up poor things.** *Poor things are poor, no matter what you want them to be.*
- **Fish or cut bait.** *If it's not working, dump it.*
- **Stop believing your own hype.** *Let your customers tell you the truth!*

Quite often I see companies who are so emotionally tied to a product or service or location that they just can't seem to bring themselves to the point of making the tough decision to dump something or someone who is not performing. In an effort to keep a pet project alive, they will start to apply cosmetic changes to real problems (i.e., lipstick on a pig). This is a recipe for disaster. Don't do it. Make the hard decision and jettison the sacred cows (pigs). Now!

Once in a while, we also see a CEO who starts to believe his company's own press. What I mean by this is that as business folks we spend so much time selling our product to anyone who will listen, that we become enamored with our own stuff beyond what is realistic. I think that this is a real "disease" among business people, and I don't think it's healthy. Over my career, I've worked with some really terrific companies, with really strong cultures; for example, PepsiCo, Price Waterhouse, and Marriott come to mind. But sometimes culture-building can go too far and the top executives become just like the story of the emperor who is wearing no clothes. Here are a couple of examples:

One company I'm familiar with has a really fabulous PR agency that continues to churn out release after release about the company and its strategy and products. The problem is that their product is really not that good, and the customers know it. But the company can't admit it. The company continues to "spin," and customers

* (Both anonymous)

continue to shake their heads, both figuratively, and literally, through their negative feedback. What the company ought to do is fix their product, and stop simply talking about it. I believe, that in this day and age, the majority of educated consumers can tell the difference between the actual "steak" and the marketing "sizzle." Concentrate on the steak. Let your ego be manifest in your exceptional service.

During the late 1990's (just before the dot-com implosion), I invested in several young companies with wonderful potential and huge promises. I even changed my career, industry, and state of residence to join an innovative start-up myself. It was a wonderfully optimistic, euphoric time in American business – but it was also a time of "glazed vision," with inexperienced, youthful CEOs unable to change course or admit failure. After three months on the job, I began to have strong reservations about the market that we were trying to serve. Seven months into my new company, I brought our executive team together and told them, "Folks, this dog won't hunt." We changed strategy immediately. I just wish I'd done it four months sooner.

On Wall Street they have an investment cliche referring to those who get too greedy in the markets: "Pigs get fat, hogs get slaughtered." In the service industries there are pig rules also. Don't put lipstick on a pig and don't try to teach a pig to sing. Listen to your customers.

Make the hard decisions about your "*pigs*." Jettison the poor products and the poorly performing employees. Do it sooner rather than later.

PRACTICAL TACTICS: (Questions to ponder)
Are you fooling yourself? Are there some products, services, or employees that you should be removing? Do the senior leaders of your company have blinders on to some "pet projects?" Do you believe your own hype? Can you make the tough decisions?

Summary

Summary

So, do you really believe? What are you going to <u>do</u> about it?

The Bible says, **"Faith without works is dead."** *
Churchill said, **"Action. This day!"** **
Yoda said, **"Do or do not. There is no 'try.'"** ***

This really isn't rocket science…and you don't need to be a brain surgeon to figure it out. Frankly, it's just about common sense, measurement, accountability, and action.

And, best of all. It works!

Two Final Examples

1. When Mindshare was rolled out to a large national restaurant chain, a very vocal, non-believing franchisee, complained loudly. His comments included, "Why do we need to measure what customers think?" And, "I don't really care about customer feedback, my customers will 'vote with their feet.'"

   Later, after using real-time customer feedback for some time, a particularly good store manager of this franchisee was promoted away from her store. Immediately there was a noticeable dip in customer satisfaction. This was followed later by a drop in customer retention and sales. Eventually, the franchisee brought the store manager back to her original post. As if on cue, satisfaction and the other metrics went right back up. He became a believer.

2. The SVP of Operations of a large quick-service restaurant chain told me about the time he realized that customer feedback really worked. There was a noticeable dip in the weekly customer satisfaction scoring trends. It was not restricted to an individual region, or market; but was across the board and could also be seen in the overall company trend line. It only lasted for one week. He sat scratching his head trying to figure out the reason for the dip. Then it dawned on him – the "down" week was the week that the company had flown all of the corporate-owned restaurant managers (GMs) to a retreat and "while the cats were away, the mice were playing." The moment the GMs got back to their restaurants, the scores spiked and started climbing again. That's when he knew, without question, that automated customer surveys provided an accurate representation of the customer experience, on a daily basis.

* (KJV: James 2:20)
** (On urgent items, Churchill would attach a note with these words)
*** (www.starwars.com)

One would be hard-pressed to find a corporate executive team that didn't advocate customer feedback and customer loyalty as an important part of their strategy. However, the implementation of that customer strategy requires *demonstrated commitment* through *resources* and *actions.*

Thank you for investing your precious resource of time in reading through these ideas. While this writing examines service as it impacts business, surely the more elevating use of service is how it can impact lives. The famous physician, philosopher, and humanitarian Albert Schweitzer said:

> **"I don't know what your destiny will be, but one thing I know: the only ones among you who will be really happy are those who will have sought and found how to serve."**

I believe that the full measure of our success is only really enjoyed when it is shared. When we use our talents and gifts to benefit others, we become truly successful.

Best of luck and success to you personally, and to your company, as you make delivering and measuring superior service the way you approach business, and life, every day.

– RDH –

Questions to Ask Yourself

1. Do we truly believe that making customers happy today, will lead to increased profits in the long-term?

2. Is the customer a primary focus of our meetings and measurement?

3. Is the importance of every employee interaction with every customer understood and reviewed regularly?

4. Do we regularly re-evaluate our products, process, and service so that we are continuously improving?

5. Do we collect real-time feedback from our customers on a continuous basis from all possible touch points (retail stores, web sites, call centers, customer care, emails, social media, etc.)?

6. Is it simple and convenient for customers to give us anonymous feedback about any part of their experience?

7. Do we integrate customer, employee, vendor, and other types of feedback together and distribute that feedback in a consolidated fashion throughout the organization?

8. Are we continuously analyzing all feedback data, watching for trends, patterns, and gaps in delivery?

9. Do we celebrate units and employees who are performing well in customer feedback metrics?

10. Are front-line and executive managers compensated on customer and employee satisfaction metrics as well as financial metrics?

11. Do we mandate participation in customer experience measurement? Or, are we sending a mixed message by presenting it as an optional program?

12. Are local managers held accountable for following up with each customer problem?

BEFORE a company commits to delivering and measuring customer service:

And AFTER:

Executive Summary

EXECUTIVE SUMMARY

> ### So, you don't feel like reading the whole book?
> ### Here's the synopsis:

COMPANY STUFF

Culture

- Focus on fundamentals: hire and teach service, hospitality, empathy, and kindness.
- Teach and practice the principle: "A complaint is a gift." Become "a culture that tolerates and learns from mistakes."
- Ask for feedback everywhere – fight fear and ego. Listen to your weaknesses.
- Hire correctly: hire employees with good attitudes. You can teach skills later.
- Get the executives off their cushy leather chairs and out on the front lines.
- Use a balanced scorecard for measurement *(i.e., financial, customer satisfaction, employee satisfaction, efficiency, and market share).*
- Encourage decision-making. Celebrate those who step up to be customer champions.
- Don't take shortcuts, they'll come back and bite you later.

Organization and Approach

- Always under-promise and over-deliver.
- Make customer feedback visible to senior management, and to line management.
- Place the customer care department high enough in the organization so that executives hear what customers are saying.
- Ensure that executives are committed to customer service and have "skin in the game" *(e.g., bonuses based on it).*
- Require team members to pass along both "good" and "bad" news as a rule.
- Remember that customer satisfaction is closely tied to and influenced by employee satisfaction.
- Take care of front-line employees, they are the face of your company.

HOW TO MEASURE

Expertise

- Use professional advisers.
- Make customer feedback measurement mandatory.
- Integrate customer feedback across all customer touch points.

Feedback

- Make it easy for customers to provide feedback.
- Provide multiple points of input for them.
- Listen to them. Really listen.
- Measure their actual experience.
- Give them what they want.
- *Respond immediately!*

Survey Methods

- Automated phone, web, and mobile-device surveys are currently the preferred collection methods *(they are real-time, anonymous, affordable, and reach your actual customers)*.
- Comment cards are slow, biased, and unreliable.
- Mystery shopping is too infrequent, too costly, and does not reflect the perceptions of your actual customers. But it does measure process and standards well.
- Face-to-face interviews (including live phone interviews) are detailed, but people are generally "conflict avoiders" and you won't get the unvarnished truth.
- Watch for new methods that may come along to supplant web and phone (IVR).

Survey Invitation

- Have the survey invitation available to customers in as many ways as possible.
- The best invitation methods are those that cannot be directly affected by the employees in any way.
- **Retail:** best practice methods include:
  - Print the invitation on the receipt (or work order) whenever possible.
  - Use numbers or bullets – set up the offer in a step-by-step outline format.
  - Keep the instructions as simple as possible – not too wordy.
  - Emphasize that the survey is quick and easy *(ex: "Take a three-minute survey")*.
  - Active solicitation methods include: e-mail and outbound telephone.

- **Call Center:** best practice methods include:
  - Calling the customer back with an automated outbound survey within minutes after the call, or
  - Before the call, using your IVR to invite the caller to stay on the line, post-call, or
  - Have the agent transfer to the survey, post-call. *(Depending upon the sophistication of your call center's infrastructure, this method might be the one you initially use until you upgrade your technology.)*

Survey Incentives

- Incentives will increase response rates and decrease some of the bias toward polarized positive and negative responders.
- Wherever possible, offer incentives that...
  - Are relevant and have broad appeal across your customer base,
  - Stimulate repeat business, and
  - Stimulate trial of strategic products or categories.
- "Soft costs" work well and are most economical.
- Dollar-denominated incentives usually work better than "% off."
- Sweepstakes incentives sometimes work; but they may skew responses toward a specific demographic.
- Survey incentives are not a stand-alone expense – they lead to increased sales and profits and should be evaluated in that context. *(i.e. show the full P & L)*

Survey Design

- Target survey length at a maximum of 3–4 minutes phone, or 5–7 minutes web *(to avoid customer survey "fatigue").*
- Concentrate on major areas you can control: people, product, environment, and processes.
- Only ask a question if the answer can drive action.
- Only include one variable per question.
- Ask open-ended questions to enhance the quantitative data results, and hear the actual "voice of the customer."

Timing of Results

- "Real-time feedback" means right now, not two weeks later when some analyst finishes a report!

How Many, How Often?

- For operations monitoring feedback, forget "sample size" – allow every single customer to respond (even ***one*** response is "valid" if you've got a dirty restroom!).
- No snapshots – take a continuous movie. Don't "start and stop" surveying.
- Target 100 customer responses per month, per "average unit."

Scoring

- Begin with the "average" scoring method. Change to a more aggressive method if unit comparisons have minimal differentiation, and if company culture and employee morale can handle the resulting lower scores. (Over-communciate!)
- Combine multiple general measures to arrive at a more stable "composite score," such as customer satisfaction index *(e.g., CSI = overall satisfaction, intent to re-purchase, intent to recommend)*.
- Focus more attention on *continuous improvement*, rather than on absolute scores.

WHY DO THIS? WHAT'S THE PAYOFF?

- Increase customer loyalty.
- Grow sales and profits.
- Deliver consistent service.
- Improve operations.
- Develop closer ties to your customers.
- Minimize risk.
- Decrease employee turnover.
- Reduce costs.

NOW WHAT?
Analyze

- Put a premium on data, measurement, and those who are good at using them.
- Measure consistency.
- Spend the effort to understand and learn. Make yours a "learning organization."
- Determine your key drivers (service areas that have the greatest impact) by deriving the relative "importance" of various attributes.
- Link customer and employee feedback to service improvement, and link service improvement to financial results.

Accountability

- Communicate results and implications.
- Deliver customer feedback down to the unit level. Establish action steps required of local managers.
- Push all results, accountability, and follow-up back to the level that delivered the service.
- Separate the content of a complaint from trying to find someone to blame.

Rewards and Punishment

- Celebrate successes and give "the carrot" equal time with "the stick."
- Reward in public. Counsel in private.
- Bonus your managers on customer satisfaction and employee satisfaction, not just on financial results (i.e. the balanced scorecard).

Action and Follow-up

- Measure trends over time.
- Develop an action plan at each retail store, field service team, call center team, and/or associate.
- Engage employees in making improvements.
- Concentrate on reducing system-wide variation between units.
- Fix problems.
- Focus on what <u>is</u> working and expand it.
- Don't "manage to exceptions."

Service-Lapse Recovery

- Solve the customer's issue. Recover them. Fix the cause.
- Preach, teach, eat, and sleep URGENCY. Recover quickly.
- Focus training on the lifetime value of each customer.
- Accept responsibility for mistakes and omissions.
- Implement service-lapse recovery for those customers who have had bad experiences. Hold local managers accountable to follow-up. Avoid permanent customer loss.
- Keep your promises! If you ask a customer if they'd like someone to call them, you'd better call them!

Miscellaneous

- Aim at 100% success – is there any goal less than perfection?
- Measure the entire customer experience, not just parts and pieces.
- Manage even trivial things that affect customers' perceptions of quality.
- Fish or cut bait. If a product, process, or person isn't working, jettison NOW!
- If you're not seeing results, check and make sure that your employees are engaged in translating measurement into action.
- Use customer voices to accentuate marketing programs. If you've been successful, tell others.

Continuous Improvement

- "Success is never final." There is no "graduation" for customer service.
- Set goals for continuous improvement.
- Lather, rinse, and repeat – this is not a trend or a fad...

...this is how you do business every day.

References and Recommended Reading

Much of my thinking on Customer Service and Customer Feedback Measurement has come from the writings of these great authors. I recommend them to you.

A Conceptual Model of Service Quality and Its Implications for Future Research
by A. Parasuraman, V. A. Zeithaml and L. L. Berry, Journal of Marketing, Fall, 1985.

A Complaint is a Gift
by J. Barlow and C. Møller, Berrett-Koehler Publishers, Inc., 1996.

Analysis of Customer Satisfaction Data
by D. R. Allen and T.R. Rao, ASQ Quality Press, 2000.

Applied Regression Analysis
by H. Smith and N. R. Draper, Wiley Interscience, 1998.

A Procedure for Identifying Value-Enhancing Service Components Using Customer Satisfaction Survey Data
by D.R. Brandt, in: Add Value to Your Service, Chicago, AMA, 1987.

Attractive Quality and Must-Be Quality
by N. Kano, et al., The Journal of the Japanese Society for Quality Control, April 1984 (orig. in Japanese).

Breaking Free from Product Marketing
by G. Lynn Shostack, Journal of Marketing, April, 1977.

Championing the Customer
by C. R. Weiser, Harvard Business Review, Dec. 1995.

Classic Failures in Product Marketing
by D. Hendon, McGraw-Hill, 1992.

Customer Experience Management: A Revolutionary Approach to Connecting with Your Customers
by B. H. Schmitt, Wiley, January, 2003.

Customer Satisfaction and Stock Prices
by C. Fornell et al, Journal of Marketing, Jan 2006.

Customer Satisfaction, Customer Retention, and Market Share
by R.T. Rust, and A.J. Zahorik, Journal of Retailing, 1993.

Customer Satisfaction Is Worthless, Customer Loyalty Is Priceless
by J. Gitomer, Bard Press, Aug. 1998.

Delivering Knock Your Socks Off Service
by K. Anderson and R. Zemke, Amacom, Jan. 1998.

Delivering Quality Service: Balancing Customer Perceptions and Expectations
by V. A. Zeithaml, A. Parasuraman, and L. L. Berry, Free Press, 1990.

Fight the Fear: The 10 Golden Rules of Customer Feedback
by B. McConnell and J. Huba, Marketing Profs, March 2004.

Firing On All Cylinders: The Service/Quality System for High-Powered Corporate Performance
by J. Clemmer with B. Sheehy, TCG Press, Apr 1992.

How Service Marketers Can Identify Value-Enhancing Service Elements
by D.R. Brandt, The Journal of Services Marketing, 2(3), 1988.

How Valuable is Word of Mouth?
by V. Kumar, J. A. Peterson, and R. P. Leone, Harvard Business Review, Oct. 2007.

Importance-Performance Analysis
by J. A. Martilla, and J. James, Journal of Marketing, 41(1), 1977.

Improving Customer Satisfaction, Loyalty, and Profit
by M.D. Johnson and A. Gustofsson, Jossey-Bass, 2000.

Improving Your Measurement of Customer Satisfaction
by T. G. Vavra, American Society for Quality, 1997.

Linking Customer and Employee Satisfaction to the Bottom Line
by D.R. Allen and M. Wilburn, American Society for Quality, 2002.

Key Driver Analysis Using Latent Class Regression
by S.M LaLonde, Eastman Kodak Company, ASA Proceedings, 1996.

Manage Your Human Sigma
by J. H. Fleming, et al., Harvard Business Review, July 2005.

Managing Brand Equity
by D. A. Aaker, The Free Press, 1991.

Marketing Services: Competing Through Quality
by L. L. Berry, A. Pasuraman, Simon and Schuster, 2004.

Measurement Scales in Consumer Satisfaction/Dissatisfaction
by D.R. Hausknecht, Journal of Consumer Satisfaction/Dissatisfaction, 1990.

Measuring Customer Satisfaction: Survey design, use, and statiscal analysis methods
by B.E. Hayes, American Society for Quality, 1998.

Moments of Truth
by J. Carlzon, Ballinger Publishing, 1987.

New Tools for Marketing Research: The Action Grid
by B. F. Blake, L.F. Schrader, et al., Feedstuff, 50(19), 1978.

Penalty-Reward Analysis with Uninorms: A Study of Customer (Dis)Satisfaction
by K.Vanhoof, et al., Intelligent Data Mining, Springer, 2005.

Putting the Balanced Scorecard to Work
by R. S. Kaplan and D. P. Norton, Harvard Business Review, Sept. 1993.

Putting the Service Profit-Chain to Work
by J. L. Heskett, W. E. Sasser, et al., Harvard Business Review, March 1994.

Raving Fans: A Revolutionary Approach to Customer Service
by K. Blanchard and S. Bowles, Harper Collins, 1993.

Revisiting Importance–Performance Analysis
by H. Oh, Tourism Management, Dec. 2001.

Services Marketing: Integrating Customer Focus Across the Firm
by V. Zeithaml, M.J. Bitner, and D. Gremler, McGraw Hill, 2003.

TARP: The Truth According to TARP
by John Goodman, Competitive Advantage, Revised Sept 2006.

The Keys to Key-Driver Analysis
by M. Hochster, ClickZ, May 2001.

The Balanced Scorecard: Measures That Drive Performance
by R. S. Kaplan and D. P. Norton, Harvard Business Review, Jan. 1992.

The Balanced Scorecard: Translating Strategy into Action
by R. S. Kaplan and D. P. Norton, Harvard Business School Press, 1996.

The Experience Economy
by B. J. Pine II and J. H. Gilmore, Harvard Business School Press, 1999.

The Importance-Performance Matrix as a Determinant of Improvement Priority
by N. Slack, Inter'l Journal of Operations & Production Management, 1994.

The Other Guy Blinked: How Pepsi Won the Cola Wars
R. Enrico and J Kornbluth, Bantam, 1986.

The Loyalty Effect: The Hidden Force behind Growth, Profits, and Lasting Value
by F. F. Reichheld, T. Teal, Harvard Business School Press, Sept. 2001.

The Mismanagement of Customer Loyalty
by W. Reinartz and V. Kumar, Harvard Business Review, July 2002.

The Service Profit Chain: How Leading Companies Link Profit and Growth to Loyalty, Satisfaction, and Value
by Heskett et al., The Free Press, April 1997.

The Service Quality Handbook
by E. E. Scheuing and W. F. Christopher, Amacom, 1993.

Total Access
by R. McKenna, Harvard Business School Press, March 2002.

Total Customer Satisfaction: A Comprehensive Approach for Health Care
by S. G. Sherman and V. C. Sherman, Jossey-Bass Publishers, 1999.

Why Satisfied Customers Defect
by T. O. Jones and E. W. Sasser, Jr. Harvard Business Review, Nov. 1995.

WWW.hotelexecutive.com: Brief portions of a few pages previously appeared in articles I wrote for **www.hotelexecutive.com.** Used with permission.

Zero Defections: Quality Comes to Services
by F. F. Reichheld and W. E. Sasser, Jr., Harvard Business Review, Sept. 1990.

Wow! A Full Page of Caveats and Disclaimers!

Credit where Credit is Due

The contents of this book are original with me, or have been collected by me over 25+ years of working in service industries. Sources have included hundreds of speeches I have attended or given and multitudes of workshops, training classes, books, and real-life experiences. I am a heavy note-taker. If I had known that someday I would be writing a book, I would have meticulously catalogued each original source at the time I collected it. But I didn't. (On the other hand, it could be argued that Adam and Eve and their family were the only ones to say anything completely original.) Nevertheless, a very lengthy and time-intensive effort has been made to track down and give attribution to original authors and source materials, but I may have missed a few. There is <u>no intent to take credit for another's work,</u> rather lack of knowledge of original authorship.

Definitions and Attributions of Evolving Terms

The internet and social media make it easy for anyone and everyone to become global authors, editors, and publishers. It also makes it very difficult to discern original authorship and standard definitions of terms. In fact, definitions of several terms I use in this book continue to change and evolve. Specific examples of this include: customer experience management (CEM), enterprise feedback management (EFM), social media, balanced scorecard, and customer recovery. (For example, one common definition of enterprise feedback management focuses on streamlining the administration of surveys, while another definition (to which I subscribe) focuses more on consolidating feedback from all sources and distributing real-time, actionable information to the accountable line manager.) Rather than list page after page of different authors and definitions in this book, I have listed one or two of the early writers on each topic. May I suggest that you do an internet search where you can view multiple claims of original authorship for multiple different definitions of the same quote or industry term.

Charts and Graphs

Each day on this planet, millions of charts and graphs are produced. The charts, graphs, and tables presented in this book are examples only, and the data in them is fictional. Any similarity between them, or their appearance, and any other presentation of data, or data itself, is 100% coincidental. To see thousands of examples of ways to present information, I suggest that you search the internet for the name of a chart type, or the analysis it portrays (e.g. "scatter plot," "matrix chart" or "importance performance analysis"). Or just search on "charts" and "graphs."

Index

Index

About the Author

RICHARD D. HANKS

Richard D. Hanks is the Chairman and President of Mindshare Technologies. Mindshare's proprietary survey and analysis technology captures customer and employee feedback in real-time and immediately transforms it into *actionable* intelligence. The company serves major clients in over 25 industries, amassing over a quarter of a billion customer insights per year. Mindshare's objective is to help its clients achieve "operations improvement through customer involvement," leading to increased customer loyalty, revenues, and profits.

Rich has been a senior executive of several Fortune 500 companies as well as several start-up ventures. He was a corporate officer at Marriott, an executive with PepsiCo and Price Waterhouse, and CEO of Blue Step, a software start-up. Rich was named "*The Leading Sales Innovator in the Lodging Industry*," and Marriott's sales team was rated one of the top 25 among all companies in the U.S. for four years under his leadership. Rich also led Marriott onto the Internet, prompting Bill Gates to refer to him as an "important Internet champion" in his book *Business @ the Speed of Thought*. Earlier in his career, Rich was called the "*Leader of Hotel Revenue Management and Strategy*" for his leadership in hotel pricing and yield management. He is also a CPA. Rich was nominated as *Utah Entrepreneur of the Year* in 2001, 2007, and 2008.

He is an author and frequent teacher/speaker at trade, academic, and professional gatherings. Rich was an adjunct professor, and taught at Cornell University for 10 years. He obtained his bachelor's degree from BYU and his MBA from Northwestern University. Rich and his wife, Liz, raised their family in Texas, Maryland, and Utah. They have three grown children, and reside in Salt Lake City. He is active in his faith, serving at various times as a missionary, youth leader, and Bishop (lay minister) of a congregation. Rich loves being with his family, and in his spare time enjoys basketball and woodworking.

Words of Wisdom

A few of my favorite quotes on delivering and measuring customer service

"A satisfied customer is the best business strategy of all." – *Michael LeBoeuf*

"It is not the employer who pays the wages. Employers handle money. It's the customer who pays the wages." – *Henry Ford*

"The Platinum Rule of Customer Service says...'Do unto others as *they* would have you do unto them.'" – *Dr. Tony Alessandra*

"Do or do not. There is no 'try.'" – *Yoda*

"I can only please one person per day. Today is not your day. Tomorrow doesn't look good either." – *Sign in a retail store*

"Confice consilium, fac velociter." (Finish planning, take swift action.)
                                        - *Mindshare Technologies Corporate Motto*

"Measure what is measurable and make measurable what is not so." – *Galileo*

"That which gets measured gets done." – *Unknown*

"Execute – Measure – Improve!" – *Unknown*

"Never underestimate the power of the irate customer." – *Joel Ross*

"Your most unhappy customers are your greatest source of learning." – *Bill Gates*

"The game of business is very much like the game of tennis. Those who fail to learn how to serve well, usually lose." – *Unknown*

"There is less to fear from outside competition than there is to fear from internal inefficiency, discourtesy, and bad service." – *Unknown*

"There are no traffic jams along the extra mile." – *Roger Staubach*

"I don't know what your destiny will be, but one thing I know; the ones among you who will be really happy are those who have sought and found how to serve."
                                        – *Dr. Albert Schweitzer*

IS YOUR CUSTOMER FEEDBACK REAL-TIME?

Which "football feedback" analogy most closely resembles your current customer experience measurement tool?

Option #1	Option #2	Option #3
Nothing	**Box Score**	**Game Headset**

NO CUSTOMER FEEDBACK	AFTER-THE-FACT RANKINGS AND REPORTS	REAL-TIME CUSTOMER FEEDBACK
Hoping and praying you get it right, or....	**Here's what you wish you'd known.**	**During the game when you need it.**
You think you already know, so why ask?	**Very little actionable information.**	**Take action as needs change.**
• Guess • Estimate • Pray • Hope • Wish • Nuthin' • Zip • Nada	• Comment Cards • Mystery Shopping • Mail-in surveys • Hotlines • Exit Interviews • Delayed data • Expensive • Not your Customer	• Real-Time • Voice of Customer • Tailored Surveys • Tailored Reporting • Cost Effective • Easy to Implement

www.mshare.net

mindshare enables...

Operations Improvement through Customer Involvement

How it works

INVITE → CAPTURE FEEDBACK → MONITOR REAL-TIME REPORTS → IMPROVE CONSTANTLY

What makes Mindshare different?

Our Approach - results oriented, operations focused.

Our People – experience and expertise, responsive, thought-leadership.

Our Technology – industry-leading: flexible, scalable, capable – easy to use.

Our Reporting - best decisions are made possible by the best information.

Mindshare's
Reporting Engine™

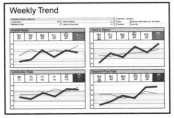

Mindshare's
Recommendation Engine™

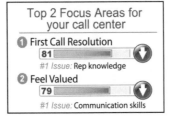

Top 2 Focus Areas for your call center

1 First Call Resolution
81
#1 Issue: Rep knowledge

2 Feel Valued
79
#1 Issue: Communication skills

Mindshare's
Text Analytics Engine™

Differentiating features and benefits

Real-time: data delivered in real-time, allowing you to respond quickly.

Enterprise feedback management: integrate feedback from all touch points, distribute immediately.

Dashboard & recommendation engine: identifies root causes and recommends solutions.

Voice/text messages: hear/read the actual customer's voice.

Instant alerts: triggered by survey responses below an acceptable range.

Tailored, hierarchical reports: specific to each organizational level.

Text analytics: sift through mounds of data to extract sentiment and meaning.

Accountability/feedback loop: enables customer service-lapse recovery.

Advanced statistics: linking feedback to financial performance!

International: 100+ countries, 25+ languages, 25 industries.

Contact us today!   **(800) 634-5407**   www.mshare.net